THIRD WAY – WHICH WAY?

How should we pay for public services?

THIRD WAY – WHICH WAY?

How should we pay for public services?

JOHN REDWOOD

MIDDLESEX UNIVERSITY PRESS

First published in 2002 by Middlesex University Press

Middlesex University Press is an imprint of
MU Ventures Limited,
Bounds Green Road, London N11 2NQ

A CIP catalogue record for this book is available from
The British Library

ISBN 1 898253 49 8

Cover Design by Helen Taylor
Manufacture coordinated in UK
Book-in-Hand Limited, London N6 5AH.

Observations on
Third Way – Which Way?

John Redwood scythes through Government spin to expose the third way for what it is: a route to expensive disappointment. In this book he applies informed economic and business ideas rather than rhetoric to the problems of how to improve Britain's public services and comes up with answers that demand attention.

Patience Wheatcroft, Business Editor, The Times

As motorists are driven off Britain's crumbling roads; frustrated train passengers struggle to cope with late-running or cancelled trains; and safety fears increase in the air and on the tracks, John Redwood sets out his blueprint for turning public services into proper services. Not so much the 'Third Way' as the right way.

Ray Massey, Transport Editor, Daily Mail

John Redwood is perhaps the most intelligent and thoughtful politician we have. He understands the realities better than almost anyone else in his profession and is unafraid to spell them out. His honesty, combined with his perceptiveness, makes his books essential reading.

Simon Heffer

One of the finest political minds of his generation, John Redwood has produced a lucid and persuasive examination of the most critical economic problem facing modern British governments: financing the public services. Taking transport as the most obvious case for treatment, he offers an analysis that is, at the same time, radical and common-sensical.

Janet Daley, Columnist, Daily Telegraph

Economic progress crucially depends on the correct allocation of tasks between government and the private sector. John Redwood makes a persuasive case for realigning present policies, giving a greater role for the private sector to achieve national objectives more effectively, particularly in the field of transport. This is no ordinary book of the "when I was in government" variety but a closely argued thesis displaying the author's unique qualifications and experience as an academic, businessman and senior politician.

Professor Sir Alan Peacock, Honorary President, David Hume Institute

John Redwood clinically dissects the myth of the 'third way'. The book is a trumpet blast of common sense, and a bold tribute to the ability of people to serve their fellow men and women for profit in ways far superior to those which can be achieved under state control or ownership."

Dr Madsen Pirie, President, the Adam Smith Institute

CONTENTS

Foreword

NO COUNTRY CAN COMPETE in today's global economy without a modern, high quality, infrastructure. Transport systems – road, rail, air and water – play a critical part in underpinning competitiveness, as do telecommunications. 'Public' services like health and education are equally important to a modern, dynamic economy.

After a long period when governments, of right and left, cut back on capital investment to minimise public spending and keep taxes low, the UK now faces major challenges. How can we find the wherewithal to modernise the UK's essential infrastructure which, by any valid comparison, is no longer fit for purpose?

There are no easy solutions to this challenge. Even with a buoyant economy, it is extremely challenging, but in times of recession or low growth, maintaining the investment required becomes almost inconceivable without massive increases in taxation. And, as demonstrated recently by the Wanless report on the funding of the NHS, and concerns about the funding of pension schemes, the UK faces these challenges with demographics that are not on our side.

Few areas of policy are more important than those which address investment in our infrastructure. The Institute of Directors has stressed the need for 'joined up' policy thinking, particularly in health care, education and transport, and for the appropriate use of markets and market-type mechanisms to achieve public policy goals. We need well-developed, rigorously evaluated, co-ordinated and innovative policy approaches.

John Redwood has long been recognised as a politician of conviction and clarity. In this latest book he develops a penetrating analysis of the failure of 'Third Way' policies to meet the dual tests of rigour and relevance. He suggests a new framework for analysing public and private activities, and for understanding the true nature of public private partnerships. By doing so, John Redwood develops a different, and critical, perspective on the increasingly complex partnership transactions that lie at the heart of 'Third Way' approaches to finance and investment.

No-one should be surprised that John Redwood argues that there should be a greater scope for the private sector in provision of

1

public infrastructure. But his reasons are not doctrinaire, they are grounded in a deep understanding of the complexities involved, and are based on clear identification and allocation of risk and return. One may or may not agree with John Redwood's prescriptions, but everyone should welcome this timely and powerfully-argued contribution to the policy debate.

Ruth Lea
Head of Policy Unit: Institute of Directors
(12 July 2002)

Introduction

IF ONLY MONEY GREW on trees all our public services could be well funded. British public debate often does not rise above the cries of the public service providers that they do not receive enough money to do the job. Traditionally opposition in the UK has centred on picking up the cries of these 'hard pressed' groups and representing them vigorously to the government until it gives in. Labour often taunted Conservative administrations on behalf of the National Health Service and social services. Conservatives often return the compliment to Labour, demanding more for the Police and armed forces.

It does not make for a particularly interesting or well-informed debate. It becomes a little more complicated when the political parties add in the vexed question of tax. The public regularly tells opinion pollsters it would like to pay more tax to finance better public services but has a strong habit of voting against parties that put higher taxes in their manifestos. The Liberal Democrats, believing the polls, have run in three General Elections on higher income tax for better schools and hospitals and three times come third. Their present policy rethink is questioning the wisdom of always being the highest tax party. The Conservatives won on lower taxes between 1979 and 1992, only to lose in 1997 because they made a mess of the economy and put taxes up despite their 1992 promises. Labour was elected in both 1997 and 2001 on a platform of no increase in taxes.

The conundrum facing democratic politicians in Britain is how to put all this extra funding into public services without having to put up taxes. A number of different ways of solving this riddle have been tried, some with some success, others with no success at all. It is the purpose of this book to look at Labour's proposed answer over the last five years: the addition of private money to public services through public private partnerships or via the Private Finance Initiative. Labour claim to have discovered a Third Way of financing public services, a perfect Nirvana where private money flows effortlessly into public services, whilst the government and public sector keeps control of the quality and quantity of service provided. As we will see, Third Way financing has come unstuck, leading to a series of disappointments and expensive mistakes for the taxpayer.

The Third Way was dreamt up by Labour policy advisers in the

3

final opposition years before their General Election victory in 1997. They called it triangulation – trying to plot a course in words and promises between free enterprise, low tax Conservatism on the one hand and full scale, high tax, planned socialism on the other. The most famous Third Way sound bite was Tony Blair's "tough on crime, tough on the causes of crime". This tried to attract both Conservative voters, who were thought to favour tough action against convicted criminals, and socialists who favoured tackling poverty, bad housing and poor schooling, things they felt caused and even in some ways excused crime. When it came to paying for public services, Labour tried to create the impression that there was a way of harnessing the private sector that fell short of privatisation, a mid-way between the state offering the service direct, and a freely competitive private sector market place. They hoped that Conservatives would like the fact that the private sector was involved and Labour would be reassured that there was no 'private sector free-for-all'. Labour wanted to pose as fiscally responsible, whilst also more generous than the outgoing Conservative Government when it came to public spending.

How can you keep taxes down whilst paying for good public services?

There are several possible ways of keeping taxes down whilst increasing the amounts spent on the most popular and politically important public services.

The first is to promote strong economic growth

This was the route tried by every post-war British government. Success in raising the growth rate helps in two direct ways. Firstly, the costs of economic failure decline. Lower unemployment means lower benefit bills. Fewer companies in difficulties means fewer demands for industrial assistance and fewer bad debts for organisations in state hands. Secondly, tax revenue grows more quickly than the economy as a whole. Incomes are taxed more heavily at the margin and, as people spend more on luxury items, so more is raised from consumption taxes. It is possible to create a virtuous circle where more money comes in, allowing more to be spent on priorities, whilst some other types of spending decline.

The second is to find reductions in spending in areas which are not priorities

The Thatcher Government between 1979 and 1990 was good at finding ways of reducing spending in certain areas both in the short term and for the longer term.

The Government made big inroads into the large industrial subsidy programmes, making the nationalised industries profitable and selling shares in them to the private sector. Instead of public industry costing the taxpayer huge sums as it had in the 1970's, the Government received large sums from share and asset sales, and then from taxation of the profitable privatised corporations.

The same Government also reformed the pensions system, encouraging many more people to make their own provision for retirement. This reduced the potential liabilities on the taxpayer by a substantial amount, projecting twenty years from the date of the policy changes.

The Labour Government came to power pledged to do something similar. They said they would cut welfare bills by promoting more jobs. As it turned out, although unemployment continued to fall under Tony Blair's first administration, total welfare bills rose as payments of other benefits increased.

The third is to charge for services that were provided free

Both the Conservative Government of John Major and the Labour Government of Tony Blair decided that students should pay for their education after the age of eighteen. The rapid expansion of numbers going on to Higher Education put strains on the budget. It means that the new generation of students will not benefit from free tuition and maintenance grants in the way previous generations did.

The previous Conservative Government introduced more charges for dentistry, moving that from a largely free service to a largely privatised one. Labour has not sought to reverse this change.

The fourth is to find private money for public service

The idea of a sharp increase in private finance for public type projects is not new. A serious interest in expanding the scope of such activity occurred in the second half of the Conservative Government from 1979 to 1997. The Government insisted that the Channel Tunnel rail link was entirely a private sector project even though the railways were still nationalised. The private sector took all the risk and soon got into financial difficulties as the cost overruns were substantial.

When it was decided to double the road capacity on the M25 over the Thames to the east of London it was agreed to do this by means of a privately financed scheme. Again, all the money raised was private and the scheme managers ran the risks. They enjoyed a toll income to pay back the capital, and then gave the new bridge to the taxpayer when they had earned sufficient to give them a return on their outlay.

Both these schemes were great successes for the taxpayer. In the one case a hazardous investment was made by the private sector. The public sector could claim credit for letting the rail tunnel be built but did not have to pay the massive bills. In the second case a low risk investment was a great success for the private sector but the public sector ended up the bigger winner with a free bridge delivered ahead of schedule. The public sector carried on collecting the tolls, even though motorists had already paid for the crossing.

Labour's Third Way finance

Seeing these successes, which looked like getting something for nothing, the new Labour Government announced that it would make a massive expansion in private finance for public projects. In particular it decided that such treatment was needed to revolutionise our creaking public transport systems. It was something that united old socialist John Prescott with new Labour Tony Blair. It was something that cheered up the politically androgynous Gordon Brown as he veered first to new Labour and then back to old, as a 'tax and spend' Chancellor. They were building such a large political tent on this issue, that done properly I would have been happy inside it as well.

This book looks at how public services are delivered in the United Kingdom. It explains that in popular language only the services that are publicly owned and run are regarded as public services but questions why that should be. Why is tube travel regarded as a public service and car travel as private? Why are the supply of bread and water private services yet the provision of some museum and library services public?

The book provides a new way of analysing services to see whether they are publicly or privately owned, whether they are monopolies or face competition and whether people pay the economic price at the point of use or pay through their taxes.

I argue that the closer we can take each service to private ownership in a competitive market, the better it will perform.

After the opening chapters examining the different types of public service and the different ways of transforming them into free enterprise success stories, the book turns to examine present government policy in the field of transport. Transport is becoming the primary battleground over Third Way finance. It has spawned a number of different and new approaches from the present Government. They are, at one and the same time, trying to change a privatised railway company into a company limited by guarantee whilst busily privatising National Air Traffic Services. They have suffered problems with financing new railway investment and their planned public private partnership for the tube is causing all sorts of technical and political difficulties. The Government has displayed muddle and lacked a sureness of touch. In some areas it is strengthening competition and private involvement, in others it condemns them and tries to recreate public monopoly.

Paying for the National Health Service
Transport is not the only area where the Government is attempting to bring in private capital. They are keen on it in the Health Service but there it is so often just an expensive way of leasing equipment or buildings. The revenue stream still comes from the taxpayer and the monopoly service calls the shots on where and when. They could, if they wished, make huge changes to the way we deliver health care in this country if they really wanted to let the private sector loose. We could have private hotels alongside NHS hospitals providing a high level of service for those patients wanting better standards of accommodation whilst giving the full clinical and medical service of the NHS free at the point of use. The private sector could supply phones, digital televisions, hairdressing, beauty treatments and other appropriate services for a fee, to brighten up life in NHS wards. The private and voluntary sectors could supply more comprehensive patient treatment in new hospitals, with NHS referrals paid for by the Government. Such changes would simultaneously increase investment, improve the range of services offered and increase the amount of private money going into health care. People paying for beds and rooms would offer more beds in each hospital and the money raised could help pay for the increased clinical activity offered free to all NHS patients, whether in a free bed or a pay bed.

Private health care is expanding quickly alongside the NHS. Most alternative medicine is provided as a fee-paying service and is becoming very popular. Sales across the pharmacy counter, self-payment for hospital treatment and insurance are all growing as people become more and more frustrated with the public offering. However, this Government is quite timid in its experiments with Third Way finance in health compared to its actions in transport preferring, in the main, a massive expansion of public spending instead for the NHS.

Consignia -Third Way for the Post Office
The Government also decided to experiment with giving greater commercial freedom to the Post Office whilst keeping it as a 100%

government owned company. The results were disastrous with the company plunging into loss and arguing against the removal of the monopoly it enjoyed over certain types of mail service. The corporation spent large sums on re-branding itself as Consignia in the hope that this would allow it to expand overseas. Instead it left it open to strong criticism as its profit and loss account deteriorated so rapidly. The Government remains embroiled in political arguments over how many post offices should remain open, as its creature tries to embark on a very large closure programme. The government has failed so far in its wish to build a People's Bank at the Post Office finding it too expensive to undertake without subsidy. The Post Office has shown that a Third Way corporation remains firmly in the public sector when it comes to paying for the losses and struggles to provide a good service to the public. Third Way at the Post Office has meant no longer paying a dividend to the Government, and cutting back on the service provided.

Transport – travelling the Third Way

This book concentrates on transport, for it is in the transport sector that the Government is showing more imagination and the private sector could make the most rapid advances without challenging the public mood. Private health care paid for by the patient still frightens many voters who accept that they should pay their train or bus fares themselves. People accept in Britain that most people, most of the time, rely on their own personalised transport to get about. Expectations of public transport have been brought low by long periods of poor performance in the public sector. A combination of low morale, poor management and "under-funding" has left us perilously short of transport capacity of all kinds. Solving the shortage is becoming crucial to success for us as a trading nation. This book examines how this could be achieved. There are chapters on railways, roads, buses and cars, canals and waterways, the London Underground and air travel.

As we will see, most of the major transport networks in this country were originally built and financed by competing companies in the private sector. Canals flourished in the eighteenth century as companies floated on the Stock Market to build them. Railways were the runaway success story of the nineteenth century, again constructed by limited liability companies, financed by share issues. The early A roads, the turnpikes, were toll financed. Only the motorway network has been paid for and built by the public sector and that remains incomplete with many obvious missing links.

Third Way finance has run into difficulties. The tube PPP is widely thought to be a very expensive way of paying for a nationalised monopoly whilst the National Air Traffic Services PPP has had to seek rescue finance just a few months after it was first established. The decision to put Railtrack into administration to try to find a Third Way vehicle to finance the railway network has, so far, proved an inglorious and expensive way of effectively nationalising the system.

We must first set out just what a public service is and analyse the different ways such services can be provided and delivered. Then we can turn to look at the practical problems and arguments over Third Way financing for the UK's ailing transport networks.

Chapter one

WHAT IS A PUBLIC SERVICE?

IN BRITISH DEBATE public service has often come to mean a service supplied to the public by the public sector. Armed with this meaning the supply of bread has never been a public service in the United Kingdom, the supply of water was a public service until the water industry was privatised, whilst the supply of security through the provision of armed forces has been a public service for a long time. Any discussion of public private partnership and how the private sector can be harnessed for the public good needs to begin with an analysis of the many different ways in which public service is provided, distinguishing between public provision and serving the public.

The complications are very obvious in the field of transport. In the United Kingdom in 2002 the provision of underground railway services in London is still a public service in all senses. The tube serves the public and the trains and track are supplied by the public sector. On the mainline railway things are less clear-cut. Travellers use private sector railway coaches running on a track run by a private sector company. This company has now been put into administration by the Government and continues with substantial public cash and direction. The aim is to establish a private sector 'not for profit' company effectively underwritten by the Government to take it over. The idea that something was either public or private and that services move from one to the other by a simple process of privatisation has been made to look old fashioned by the enormous complexity of Third Way politics and economics. This has produced a whole series of hybrids entailing partial private provision, sub-contracted private provision, partnership provision and a mixture of financing systems.

The three criteria for defining a public service

At the most general level all services offered to the public, whether by the private or public sector, are public services. The supply of bread is as much a public service as the supply of tube travel and at least as important. In both cases members of the public pay willingly to enjoy the benefit of the service but in the one case they can choose

10

their loaves from a variety of private sector providers competing on price and quality whereas in the other, tube travel, it is a take it or leave it offering. There are three central questions to be asked to get a clearer view of the true nature of any particular public service. Firstly, is it a service supplied by a monopoly or by the competitive market place? Secondly, is the good or service supplied free at the point of use, or with some element of public subsidy at the point of use, or does the customer or client pay the economic price when he or she chooses the service? Thirdly, does the public sector wholly or partially provide the service or is it entirely supplied by private sector companies financed by private money?

These three questions enable us to group public services into the eight broad categories outlined below. There are four different types of monopoly service and four different types of competitively provided service.

Completely public sector activities (public monopolies)
These are the activities that the public most clearly identifies with the government and understands as being pure public services. There is no choice over their supply; people pay through general taxation and public sector employees deliver the services. The best example is the employment of the armed services. It is generally agreed in the British debate that we do not wish to license or approve private armies and that collective security is best supplied by the government with the necessary democratic protections in place over its use. It would not be practical to send people regular bills claiming that they had used a certain amount of defence over the previous month; it is much easier to pay out of general taxation.

In the United Kingdom there have been a large number of services in this category since the end of the Second World War. Most of our health care is delivered by a public sector monopoly employing health staff and delivering most of the health care free at the point of use. There has been some erosion with the introduction of charges for ophthalmic and dentistry services and through modest growth in a private competing sector but, by and large, our Health Service still falls in this public sector category. A great deal of our education is similarly delivered with modest competition from the private sector available only to those on high incomes. Charges have been introduced only at the periphery for after school activities, school trips, some extra curricular activities and the like. There has been little choice or competition in education with most people having to accept the neighbourhood primary school and then the neighbourhood comprehensive for their child. In some areas there is scope for choice between comprehensives and, in counties like Kent and Buckinghamshire, there remains the option of grammar school education.

Monopoly public services paid for by the public but provided by the private sector (contracting out)

The most famous example of contracting out came in the 1980's with the development of the idea that refuse services for domestic households could be more cheaply and effectively delivered by private sector companies than by council workforces. The traditional model was similar to the National Health Service or the Army but organised at local government level. Domestic refuse collection was a monopoly. The public did not pay for their household refuse collection specifically at the point of use but made a contribution through their rates. The vehicles were owned by the local council and the dustmen employed by local government.

In the 1980's, it was decided to establish some kind of competitive check on the levels of efficiency and cost of council provided services. In many parts of the country private sector contractors were able to offer a similar level of service to that supplied by the council workforce at a lower price. In some cases there were poor working practices that could be eliminated, in other cases the application of better management and technology could produce a cheaper answer.

Although many traditional public sector workers have been very hostile to the idea of contracting out it has been remarkable how keen senior grades of civil servant are on contracting out for many of their own activities. In recent years, in both local and central government, we have seen a spate of consultancy contracts awarded to give national and local government advice on a whole series of policy issues and problems formerly analysed and handled by the civil service. Government has got used to turning to the private sector for a wide range of services. Much of the Government's publicity and advertising is undertaken by private sector contractors. The Government will turn to private sector head hunters and employment agencies for recruitment, to bankers and financial advisers on a range of financing issues and to specialist companies to run leisure facilities, conferences, catering and cleaning. A large market place has been created for the private sector to do everything from supplying the civil servant with a cup of tea and washing up the cups, through to telling the government how to sort out the railway.

In the case of refuse, the service to business is organised on a different basis. Businesses are required to pay the economic price of their refuse collection and have a choice of contractor to carry out the task. Refuse services are provided free at the point of use by a local monopoly for the residential customer. Conversely, business refuse collection is provided by an entirely competitive market based service, often with a public sector option when choosing who best to carry out the task.

Monopoly services paid for by the private sector but provided by the public (regulatory bodies)

Many licensing and regulatory areas fall into this category. The public is expected to pay at the point of use but the service is supplied as a monopoly by the public sector. One of the most obvious examples is planning. People have no choice over who is going to award them planning permission, having to go to the relevant planning authority in the area where they wish to undertake the development. Most planning activities are provided within the planning authority which employs specialist staff to prepare advice, seek the decision of the planning committee and to send out the decision letters. It is true that there is now substantial contracting out in this area to private sector planning lawyers but the typical extension, new garage or conversion of the domestic house is usually handled entirely by public sector staff employed by the local council.

The growth of regulation in recent years has been rapid. At the same time, there have been quite sharp increases in fees for many of the regulatory services provided. Until recently National Air Traffic Services was in this category. A monopoly service provider took responsibility for guiding the planes across British airspace, to and from the airports of their choice. Public sector employees provided the service as a monopoly with fees charged to the airlines based on their usage. The decision to create a public private partnership out of National Air Traffic Services caused a number of surprises. Many people feel that a regulatory service like this has many of the characteristics of a natural monopoly. In the interests of public safety the state naturally insists on airlines using the system, so many argued it made sense to keep the whole thing under public sector control. Others in the debate saw that it is possible to handle services like this in the private sector subject to certain controls.

The reason the Government wanted to move the service into the private sector was capital financing. National Air Traffic Services was entering a cash-hungry period, needing substantial sums of money to update the technology of its system and expand its capacity to handle the growing surge in air travel. Critics of the scheme produced two objections in principle. The first was the danger of over-pricing. This question need not be an insuperable difficulty when wishing to privatise a service of this nature. It is quite possible to put in place a control on the regulator, limiting the increases in fees or charges by some formula, which can be cost related. Such controls can also include an incentive for the privatised service to improve its productivity and efficiency year by year. The second issue raised was safety. There are some proponents of public sector service provision who worry that the private sector would be reckless with safety, putting profit before caution. This has always seemed to me to be an unreasonable allegation. Most people working in the competitive private sector are well aware that if they jeopardise safety and get a reputation for cutting corners on this important matter they will soon be driven out of business completely. Airlines face cut throat competition and remorseless pressure to lower their seat prices as people are always looking for cheaper tickets. They also know that if they economise too much on safety and have one or more bad crashes it would be extremely difficult to persuade people back onto their airline.

The early days of the Government's public private partnership for National Air Traffic Services produced a different kind of problem altogether. The Government decided to retain a 49% shareholding, sell 46% to a consortium of airlines and leave the balancing 5% in the hands of the employees. It did not create a strong enough balance sheet to support the large capital expenditure programme NATS had to follow. Financial difficulties soon hit owing to the collapse in air travel following the terrorist attack on the World Trade Centre on 11 September 2001. As NATS revenues were entirely dependent upon the number of planes flying into and out of the leading airports in the United Kingdom, it found it very difficult to handle the decline in revenues. It had to go back to both the private sector and the government to seek more money. Critics of the scheme from both sides of the argument felt they had been vindicated. To all those supporters of the public provision of public services it was proof that the private sector was unable to handle the first downturn that had occurred and immediately wanted public subsidy to keep it going. To supporters of the full private provision of services it demonstrated that a compromise position, without a strong balance sheet and without clarity over who would pay in the event of something going wrong, was an accident waiting to happen.

It will be interesting to see whether the experiment with hiving-off regulatory type activities from the state to the private sector is one that either the United Kingdom government or governments elsewhere decide to persevere with. There will always be problems because, by definition, these regulatory services are monopolies and people in businesses are sometimes reluctant purchasers of their service. These issues can be tackled by proper monopoly regulation, bringing the possibility of gains from private sector management and from private sector finance if well handled.

Monopoly services paid for by the private sector and provided by the private sector (private monopolies)

It is the ambition of many successful business people to build monopolies for themselves. The monopoly business has the advantage of dictating to customers the range and quality of the product or service offered as well as substantial pricing powers. For this reason it has been a long-standing feature of American and, more recently of European law that wherever possible, monopolies be resisted, prevented or broken up. There are very few natural monopolies, far fewer than people often suppose. In the United Kingdom it has regularly been claimed that the provision of water services is a natural monopoly. This is based upon the proposition that someone has to own a pipe network with pipes going to every household and he who owns the pipe network, therefore, has monopoly control over the service. There is absolutely no reason why this should be so. There are many examples around the world of pipeline networks being used as common carriers allowing a range of service providers to send their product through the pipes. There are also many examples globally of private sector companies thinking it worthwhile to duplicate pipe networks or put in new elements to existing pipe networks under different ownership. Gradually, in the United Kingdom, the Government and regulatory authorities are coming to see that water could be as competitive an industry as the provision of gas, electricity or phones, all requiring channels to individual houses. There is considerable scope for water provision from boreholes, river and canal extraction and collection in situ, as well as reservoir water supplied through a pipe network.

Competition law attempts in the major jurisdictions to prevent the creation of monopolies by merger and acquisition. Once a company gets a market share, usually one quarter, it becomes extremely difficult or impossible to add to that market share by the purchase of other competing businesses. Competition law also prevents cartelisation: the decision of competing businesses to gang up on the customers by agreeing a policy on pricing, range and quality of good or service offered. Heavy penalties are imposed in the United States and Europe on all found offending against these rules.

It is possible to build up a monopoly by developing a new product or service and being very good at its provision. United States Anti-Trust law has just been wheeled out against Microsoft for doing just this. Microsoft developed a software package, an entirely new area of activity and was most successful in making it the world standard for a whole variety of PC's and computer systems. US authorities are now seeking to make it easier for competitors to challenge this strong market position established by the world leader.

In the United Kingdom the principal monopolies are ones created by the state. The best example of a monopoly private sector service paid for privately is the provision of Railtrack by the eponymous company. Railway services used to be supplied by a monopoly public service. The competing train companies of the pre-war period had been bought up at the taxpayer's expense by the post-war government and remained as an operating rail monopoly combining track, trains and signals under single ownership until rail privatisation in the 1990's. During that privatisation the Government decided that the provision of train services would be made more competitive by the award of franchises after competitive bidding but also determined that the provision of the track should remain in single private sector ownership. This entailed regulation to make sure that Railtrack plc did not simply cover any costs it wished to incur and make large profits by putting up the charges to the train companies for using the track supplied.

Motorway service areas have some similar elements. The facilities are now provided by a variety of competing companies but in any given place, given the planning restrictions on the number of motorway services areas, a motorway service facility has an effective monopoly. For this reason the Government introduced a franchising process, imposing regulatory requirements on the service provided. The construction of more motorway service areas would reduce the monopoly elements but is not thought acceptable in many parts of the country given the amount of land that would be taken up by such a development.

Competitive services paid for by the public sector and provided by the public sector (local public services)
The public sector is reluctant to compete against itself for both good

and bad reasons. Many opponents of competition argue that the public sector ethos, based on serving the public in a reputable and caring way, would be undermined if competition were introduced. Trade unions are very reluctant to see competition introduced in the public services, as they fear it might eliminate certain working practices and might serve to lower rates of remuneration in some cases.

Others see the advantages of competition. A friendlier word for competition is choice. There are some limited examples of this appearing in the United Kingdom public sector.

Perhaps the best example is the provision of general practitioner services. Most local areas have more than one general practice and within the practice there is often a choice of doctor. The choice of doctor is often a very personal one with some women, for example, preferring a female GP. The relationship between the GP and the patient can be very important if the patient needs to make regular visits. It is a relationship based on trust. For this reason patients in a free service have limited rights to ask for a transfer of GP if they are not happy with the service being provided.

In some parts of the country, for some people, there is a similar choice with schools. In suburban or urban areas parents of primary school children do often have a choice of two or three schools. Many parents concerned about the education of their children take the duty of choosing seriously. They will visit each of the schools, read the annual records and talk to parents and children involved. In some cases the choice also extends to secondary school although in many parts of the country the choice is between different comprehensives rather than a more fundamental choice between different styles of school. The previous Conservative Government tried to move in the direction of offering more real choice: establishing city technology colleges, keeping the grammar schools that still remained and urging local authorities to give more parents more opportunity to choose between the different schools in their area. As Secretary of State for Wales responsible for education in the principality, I launched an initiative called Popular Schools. This gave the money to schools that were attracting a large number of applicants to build the extra classroom, expand the other facilities and recruit the extra teachers needed so that more places could be created at the schools that people liked most.

Overall policy control and guidance of the public sector is committed to elected Members of Parliament and Councillors. In a way this is the ultimate example of the competitive provision of publicly provided and publicly paid for service. Every four or five years people in every part of the country have the opportunity to pass judgment on the quality of service and the range of views expressed by their local parliamentary representative. Similarly, at regular intervals in each Unitary Council, Borough, District and County area, people have the opportunity to pass judgment on the quality of service and the wisdom of guidance offered by their local councillors.

In some cases 'free' services provided by the public sector compete against paid for services in the private sector. This is particularly true in the leisure area. Subsidised or free swimming pools, athletics tracks and playing fields compete against often much more expensive facilities offered in the private sector. Owners of existing private sector facilities can become understandably upset if the public sector suddenly decides to introduce a heavily subsidised competitor when their business plans have been based on the assumption that they were operating in a leisure area where people would pay at the point of use.

Competitive services paid for by the public sector but provided by the private sector

The public sector buys a great deal from the private sector and nearly always buys it through a competitive tendering process to ensure the right quality at the lowest price. A good example of such a service in action is the provision of residential and nursing care home places. The state accepts responsibility for people with low incomes and few assets if they need residential or nursing care in their old age. In recent years an increasing number of such elderly people are being placed in private sector care homes by the public sector, their fees being paid through the local council . This situation has evolved from one where many councils had their own public sector homes to meet the requirements of their elderly people.

The present UK Government is considering introducing something similar alongside the NHS. In a limited number of cases the NHS uses public money to buy an operation or treatment at a private clinic or hospital in Britain or abroad. The private sector has to offer a competitive package and the public sector pays the bill.

Competitive services paid for privately but provided by the public sector (municipal or government trading)

These used to be much more numerous than they are today. They were by definition the easiest government services to privatise completely. The Conservative Government of 1979 to 1990, led by

Margaret Thatcher, was an enthusiastic privatiser of such activities. Shares in British Petroleum, the whole of Amersham International, Cable & Wireless, the British National Oil Corporation and a range of transport and energy businesses were sold from the public sector to the private sector. Today such activities are more likely to be found at the local government level. Councils often provide refuse services to businesses and leisure facilities in competition with the private sector. At the national level the last remaining big example is the Post Office. Although the central business, the letter monopoly, is not open to competition the Post Office also runs competitive parcels and time sensitive mail services where there is vigorous permitted competition from private sector competitors.

The Post Office has been through a metamorphosis under the present Labour Government. Renamed Consignia, it has seen some limited additional operating freedoms which fell far short of what the board were seeking. The Government has decided to change the arrangements for the payments of benefits to many people, undermining one of the important sources of business and revenue to Post Office Counters throughout the country. For this and other reasons, the Post Office has moved from profit into loss and is now becoming a problem for the Government, making claims on public expenditure after many years of making a contribution. Under European Union guidance and control, competition is being introduced into the principal letter monopoly. This too will then become a competitive business with a substantial proportion of the service provided by a publicly owned organisation. Pressure will undoubtedly mount for the whole thing to be privatised as competition is introduced. It will become more and more difficult to understand why the public sector is running the financial and management risk in what will then be a proper competitive market.

Competitive services paid for privately and privately provided (the norm in most areas)

This is usually the best solution for most types of good and service provision. The big privatisation movement of the 1980's has made it the norm in many areas of life. In the 1960's and 1970's, the United Kingdom had something called the mixed economy, ranging from completely publicly financed services at one end of the spectrum through nationalised monopoly provision, to a private competitive market at the other end. The middle area has been very squeezed by the privatisation movement. It is now the case that most of our transport, energy, all of our telecommunication services, and water are now supplied by competitive companies in the private sector.

Before this they were supplied by state run monopolies. Many areas of life have always been privately provided through fierce competition. Housing for sale, housing for rent for most periods of our history, food, clothing and other essentials have usually been supplied by freely competing private sector organisations and companies.

It is very difficult for a public monopoly to make good decisions about technology and capital investment. The private competitive market place is restless with people constantly trying out new ideas, seeing what works best. In the public sector with monopoly provision very large and fundamental decisions have to be taken. This tends to encourage considerable caution and may, from time to time, involve making a large decision which is wrong, pushing the British activity down a cul-de-sac or into a blind alley. When telephones were provided in Britain by a monopoly public sector provider, the UK was very late in moving away from mechanical to electronic technology. The UK decided to move to an intermediate system of switching called TXE4. This left the British supplying industry manufacturing equipment that proved impossible to sell elsewhere in the world. When the industry was privatised there was a process of accelerated investment in electronic switching and, more recently, in a move from analogue to digital transmission.

In the public sector it is difficult to get these decisions right. There is not the same capacity to innovate and experiment and there is no market test to see whether another system might have been better. There are also considerable constraints on the amount of money available at any given time for investment. The telephone industry in the 1970's and early 1980's was always battling with the Treasury to try and get permission to borrow or raise more capital to accelerate expansion and modernisation of the network. Once the industry was privatised the capital shortage was removed. Indeed, at the end of the 1990's, the private sector rather overdid capital provision to the telecommunications industry.

The private sector has shown itself capable time and again of developing new technologies rapidly and letting the market decide which are the best. In recent years we have seen an explosion of new technologies for communicating messages and relaying music and film. If this industry had been organised as a public sector monopoly it is extremely unlikely that all these different technologies would have been tried out. It is even more unlikely that the public would have been able to choose which they preferred and to influence the lines of development of music, film, messaging and personal computing. Huge sums of money have been released from the private market place for all these developments. Large sums of money have been tried out and wasted. Other businesses have been more successful, making large fortunes for their founders and their early backers. It all seems very remote from the arguments of the early 1980's about how in Britain we could afford to finance the next generation of switchgear for traditional landline telephones and the discussions about whether a new channel could be permitted in the strictly controlled and partially state run broadcasting system.

Shifting the balance between the different types of finance and management

A number of initiatives have been launched to change the boundaries between these different categories of activity. Under the Conservative Governments of 1979 to 1997, there were four particular sets of policies designed to shift the balance away from monopoly, publicly provided, publicly paid for services towards rather more competitive, privately paid for, privately provided services.

Privatisation

The first of these was the policy of privatisation. Privatisation is a policy designed to switch the ownership of service provision from the state to private individuals and/or companies. There were many examples during the Conservative years of successful privatisations, selling the assets to a very wide variety of new owners. In some cases the state sold shares to a large number of new shareholders who could actively trade them on the Stock Market. The large-scale privatisations of British Telecom, British Gas and British Airways created large private sector companies with hundreds of thousands of private shareholders and professional management. In other cases the shareholdings were sold to trade buyers or to employees. National Freight Corporation was sold to its managers and employees who went on to transform its fortunes and turn it into a very profitable, fast growing and successful business.

Competition

The second policy pursued was breaking monopolies. Very often breaking the monopoly had a bigger impact upon the conduct of the former public sector service than transfer of ownership. It was competition which brought in a stimulus to thinking, forced the former monopoly into improving its efficiency, lowering its prices, extending its range of goods and services on offer and improving its technology. Gradually the monopolies of British Telecom, British Gas and the old electricity industry were broken. New challengers emerged supplying cheaper telephone calls, cheaper gas and cheaper electricity and offering more flexible packages and a wider range of service to the customers.

Contracting out

The third policy was to introduce substantial contracting out. Where it wished a service to be publicly paid for, supplied by the public sector, usually a local council, it required the provision of such service to be put out to tender. This process tested whether a private sector company or companies could perform it better and more cheaply than the in-house team delivering the service up to that point. In areas like cleaning, catering and refuse collection the private sector made rapid strides in taking over from municipal activity. In each case the savings were real and, in many cases, quite substantial. Typically the cost of the service was reduced by about a quarter as a result of successful contracting out.

Liberalisation.

The fourth policy was that of deregulation or liberalisation in a number of areas, permitting new activities to take place that were previously banned by law and permitting new entrants to emerge in areas which had previously been the prerogative of a public sector monopoly or dominant player. In the telecommunications industry, for example, the Government held successive licensing rounds to encourage new companies to provide telephone services. A Government decision to licence new users of the radio spectrum led to the development of a whole range of mobile telephone services that simply did not exist before this liberalisation. Similarly, it was a Government decision to allow a commercial satellite challenge to the established duopoly of the British Broadcasting Corporation and Independent Television, to bring to Britain multi-channel television which the United States of America had enjoyed for many years.

Each of these policies changed the balance of the British economy moving more services from monopoly to competitive markets and more services from public provision to private provision. The Government was much more reluctant to shift activities from free public provision at the point of use to private payment.

User charging

The Government always understood that this was likely to prove unpopular and in the limited number of cases where it was attempted, so it proved. The Government did introduce a wider range of charges for dentistry and ophthalmic work in the National Health Service. Labour opposition at the time bitterly opposed the introduction of charges for eyes and teeth, even though there were substantial and generous exemptions for anyone on a low income or no income. It has been interesting to notice, however, that in the five years of Labour administration there has been no attempt to reverse this policy in England and Wales. The Conservative Government introduced charges for museums, which again were bitterly opposed and where the incoming Labour Government did, after a pause, decide to reintroduce free visits to museums in a number of important cases.

All major parties have accepted the fundamental principle of the NHS that those needing access to clinical or medical treatment, whether on an emergency basis or not, should receive the treatment free at the point of use whatever their income based only on an assessment of their medical needs. Similarly, all political parties have accepted that education should be provided free of charge for children in the age range five to eighteen, with the political parties entering a kind of auction to see how far they can go in offering free education to the under fives as well. Both the Conservative and Labour administrations of the 1990's decided that students over the age of eighteen should make a bigger contribution to their own costs. The Conservative Government introduced student loans to take care of part of the maintenance costs of each student and the Labour Government has followed that up with an introduction of some element of tuition fee as well. It seems likely that these trends will continue, with the tax payer being invited to assume more and more of the costs of early education and child care for the under fives, whilst students will be asked to assume a bigger and bigger proportion of the burden of the costs of educating themselves between the ages of eighteen and twenty-two. There has been a long debate about residential and nursing home provision. The cross party consensus that elderly people should pay if they have the means is under pressure to move to a more generous system.

One of the big debating issues with public provision is to what extent if any it should be extended when the private sector proves itself more adept at developing new services and offering them to the public. In the case of health there is now an active debate about whether the NHS should offer the alternative and herbal therapies and remedies that are popular and common in the private sector. There has been a strong growth in therapies like acupuncture and massage for orthopaedic and stress-related problems and there has been a growing tide of enthusiastic support for herbal remedies for a whole variety of complaints. Some believe that these remedies should also be available through the NHS, some even arguing they might offer a more cost effective and satisfactory way of dealing with the underlying medical problems. Others believe that the NHS should remain wedded to chemical based medicine drawing on the strong links between the pharmaceutical companies and the NHS in its current form. The truth probably lies somewhere between the two. In some cases it may be that alternative therapies offer a cheaper and better way of dealing with something that the NHS is already tackling through the application of drugs. In other cases the private sector is probably offering a treatment or facility that is not available at all on the NHS and would therefore be an additional cost on the system.

It shows how complex these matters are even in an area where British people would intuitively think that all was provided free at the point of use by a comprehensive national system. People are learning about their NHS that there are very clear boundaries and limits to what it can and does do. People are used to treating themselves over the counter in the local pharmacy for a whole variety of minor conditions and ailments. All of us think it perfectly reasonable that, if we cut our finger, we should buy a plaster from the chemist and deal with the problem ourselves. Many of us think it reasonable if we get a cold or flu not to trouble the doctor but to buy a suitable remedy from the local pharmacy and try to cure ourselves. In this respect we are happy with profit-maximising companies offering private sector services to deal with our day-to-day health ailments.

Public private partnership

It is into this complex world that the Labour government has injected the idea of public private partnership. It is not an entirely new idea. It is new language for a rather old idea of the public and private sectors working together in a variety of ways. The private contractor offering the refuse service in a local authority area is an example of a public private partnership. So too is an elderly person in a private sector residential care home paid for by the state. A number of leisure projects have been developed over the years as joint use projects. They may entail a 'for profit' element with private sector management and full charges for certain users at certain times of day. Other money is put in by the local council for school and social service use of the same facility.

What the new Labour Government had in mind in coming to power in 1997 was to offer reassuring language to the public sector trade unions whilst, at the same time, finding mechanisms for harnessing private sector management and finance in a range of public sector activities. It was looking for a third way – not capitalism, not socialism, not full privatisation, not traditional public sector provision. It had big ambitions for modernising and 'investing' in a range of public services. It recognised that there were problems in the way the old public sector organised itself and it saw the financial difficulties of raising the huge sums of money needed to improve areas like transport, leisure and health, without bringing in substantial money that did not count as direct public spending.

The difficulties have arisen through lack of clarity and through the battle going on in the governing party over what they are trying to do. Whilst the modernisers in Labour are genuinely relaxed about the private sector having a much bigger role, taking more risk and in return getting some reward, there are many others inside and influencing the Labour Government, who hanker after a more traditional public sector model with public sector control. Some in the Government have seen the role of the private sector like that of a leasing organisation. They hoped that they could find private finance for a whole series of public sector projects, which would remain more traditional public sector projects in many other ways. They discovered that the problem with this route was that it was just an expensive way of the Government borrowing and nothing real had been achieved in terms of transferring risk. Others in the Government were more open minded and saw the need to transfer some risk to the private sector but found it difficult to go far enough to make it worthwhile for the extra cost entailed. As we will see, the result was endless delay and recourse to very large numbers of private sector advisers and consultants to try and hammer out a sensible compromise position. Well over £100 million was spent on consultancies to try and work out a public private partnership model for the London Underground system. Now at least as much is likely to be spent on trying to work out a model for restructuring a private sector Railtrack that is more under the control of the government than the old Railtrack plc. Consignia dipped into losses shortly after the reorganisation as a Third Way corporation with more commercial freedom but still in public ownership. NATS rapidly required a large capital injection after its establishment as a more independent public private partnership. Neither of these has augured well for the process. It is now our task to turn to look at the role of these public private partnerships, to examine how they might evolve and to see why we need very large sums of additional private money to improve our transport and health systems.

Chapter two

PUBLIC MONOPOLIES DO NOT SERVE US WELL

A TRADITIONAL PUBLIC SERVICE offers a monopoly that is run, directed and managed by the public sector. It is a service supplied by public service employees who direct and run it under the more or less watchful eye of elected politicians in a democratic state like the United Kingdom. A large number of advantages are put forward for such a system but experience shows the results are far from the ideal set out by public sector theories.

THE ADVANTAGES OF PUBLIC MONOPOLIES

It is said that keeping a service as a monopoly enables the monopolist to reap the economies of scale. The opportunity to plan provides a more rational and efficient delivery of service than a competitive market could provide. Wasteful competition is eliminated and the money that would otherwise have been spent on competitive advertising can in theory be spent on the service itself. The monopoly permits an integrated network. It should be capable of putting safety before profits, taking care of the environment, creating an equal service throughout the country and offering a good deal including stable employment to the employees. Some argue that many such public services are natural monopolies needing public sector involvement to tame them. In some cases the provision of a public monopoly enables the government to supply more of the good or service to a better standard than the market itself would provide, with the government judging that this is in the interests of the electorate.

The economies of scale

In services like the provision of electricity, gas or water there should be substantial economies of scale. It should be cheaper to generate electricity from very large plants or power stations. It should be cheaper to collect large quantities of water in a given location and route them around the country from there, rather than having segregated water collection in small quantities at many locations. It should be cheaper for one large organisation to have one board of directors and one central team than to allow dozens of smaller companies to emerge, each with a need for some centralised control and expertise.

It is possible to see the economies of scale very clearly in the transport industries. If a service provider has a limited volume of goods to send he often has to rely on very expensive postal or hand deliveries. As he builds up the size of his business he can afford his own van, lowering the unit cost of the transport for his operation. As he grows in scale again he may be able to buy a fleet of lorries and, when he really hits the big time, he can negotiate the cheapest possible contracts for rail, ship or lorry transportation of his goods. The more service he buys the cheaper it becomes. The larger he is the more chance he has to run his own operation as a competitive check on the market place itself. The bigger he is the more feasible it is to switch between different methods of transport depending on relative costs and convenience.

This argument has been used constantly to reinforce the monopolistic tendencies of public service provision. We were told when we had a nationalised electricity industry that large, coal-fired power stations were the cheapest and best way of generating the power. Once the monopoly was broken the industry changed its methods of generation dramatically, with the private sector competitors immediately wanting to introduce combined cycle gas technology, which greatly lowered the cost of production. The size of plant was far less important than the fuel and the technology used. The nationalised gas monopoly was very reluctant to gather gas from the North Sea in the early days of its production. Once the private sector challenge was introduced everyone realised that North Sea natural gas had to be collected and was a cheap option.

In each case where monopolies were broken in the public service, far from the costs going up, with the introduction of competitors the costs and the prices came down. The reduction in telephone prices was dramatic. The reduction in electricity and gas prices is still continuing but has also been impressive. There is no case, so far, of competition removing the economies of scale in a way which damages the customer. It has been discovered in most cases that the diseconomies of large monopolistic organisations have nearly always been greater than the economies of scale that these companies have been able to enjoy. Indeed, one might argue more convincingly that the nationalised monopoly is the best means so far invented to offset the economies of scale in a large organisation.

Public monopolies eliminate wasteful competition

The idea of wasteful competition is an economic nonsense. In free market theory inefficiencies get competed out in the market place. If there is an optimum size of a plant or an optimum scale of a company operating in a free market then companies will tend towards that technology and that size. It is only when governments intervene that this process is impeded or prevented. Public sector apologists believe that a competitive market encourages waste. They say that far too much is spent on advertising, promotion and on company hierarchies and superstructures.

The problem with the public monopoly response is that this usually encourages a wasteful attitude towards public money. Indeed, it is safer to say that public monopoly enterprise encourages wasteful expenditure of money on a much greater scale than competition encourages waste. The public enterprise does not eliminate the need to spend money on advertising, promotion and marketing. However big the public monopoly is it will still have competitors or a challenge at its boundaries or margins. In the days when Britain had a monopoly electricity and a monopoly gas industry they felt they needed to compete in the fuel market and certainly needed to compete against the private sector competitors supplying oil based products. This required substantial expenditure on advertising making the claim for their fuel. They also acknowledged that advertising, marketing and promotion has a very important role to play in presenting customers with information. An electricity monopoly needs to tell its customers how to obtain a supply, how to remedy faults, how to pay their bills and where to obtain their electric appliances.

There are fewer advantages from having fewer senior managers as well. Whilst it is true that there are fewer board directors with a public monopoly than with a range of competing companies, a public enterprise monopoly usually has many layers of management offsetting the possible advantages in costs that could accrue from the elimination of extra jobs at the top. Public monopolies usually become rigid bureaucracies with minute differentiations or divisions of labour between the many competing grades of manager. On privatisation, substantial changes are normally made to the hierarchies of these organisations, with a view to increasing responsibility and accountability and reducing the cost of intermediate management.

Public monopoly brings the advantages of planning
In theory making one set of rational decisions for the provision of say telephone services or electricity in a country the size of the United Kingdom should bring considerable advantages. Many

apologists for planning argue it is far better than relying upon the chosen actions of myriad different players seeking to make their impact upon the local, regional or national economy. The problem with monopoly planning is that the people in charge can often get it wrong. Single decision taking at the top can be so much more dangerous for the industry and the country than varied decision taking by a number of different companies and players in a competitive market place.

If one electricity generation company makes the wrong decision about which plant to buy, all that will happen is that that company's market share will contract and its rivals will gradually displace it. If the government and the directors of a nationalised monopoly make a wrong decision about which kind of electricity to buy then the whole country will be saddled with the consequences of that decision for many years to come. One way or another, British consumers and British industry will have to pay the extra costs of the decision. It may be done through taxation and subsidy but it may be done directly by charging customers a higher price than those using rival systems abroad.

Nationalised monopolies in Britain were extremely good at getting big decisions wrong, offsetting the possible advantages of planning. The nationalised electricity industry did decide to concentrate its fuel power on coal-fired power stations. These stations were only 33% to 35% fuel efficient, compared with the 60% fuel efficiency of combined cycle gas stations and the 75% or 80% fuel efficiency that can be obtained from combined heat and power schemes. Throughout the post war nationalised era the industry pushed on with its coal generation strategy, lumbering Britain with a less efficient and more expensive system of power.

The telecommunications industry went one better and did even more damage to its supplying industry at the same time as leaving Britain with a very inadequate telecommunications system. It carried on buying mechanical exchanges long after electronic systems had found their way into overseas jurisdictions. It forced the British supplying industry into designing and marketing the Strowger and TXE4 systems at a time when the international market wanted something more sophisticated. The supplying industry found it very difficult to compete abroad when its large monopolistic domestic market had such idiosyncratic and outdated requirements. The British telephone customers suffered, as the network was not up to the requirements of modern systems, whilst the supplying industry suffered having to divert so much of its energy into what turned out to be largely unsaleable equipment for the global market place.

Once the telecommunications industry was privatised and the monopoly broken, there was a revolution. The industry immediately went over to electronic modern switching systems capable of handling sophisticated data as well as voice traffic. The privatised industry set about expanding capacity by the leaps and bounds needed. It also released the energies of the supplying industry, which started to strengthen as soon as the dead hand of monopoly procurement was lifted from the UK economy.

Public monopoly provides an integrated network which brings great advantages

Rational planning on a nationwide scale should bring substantial advantages in terms of a smooth running, integrated network across the country as a whole. This should be most pronounced in something like the railway industry where the government has most of the advantages. For 50 years after the Second World War, the state in Britain owned the track, the trains and the signals, employed all the railway men and of course also had its own planning powers and its ability to acquire land by compulsory purchase. This formidable array of instruments should have allowed the state to build an integrated modern national railway network capable of serving the transport demands of the public. However, for a variety of reasons the public monopoly failed to do this.

One single best example of the railway industry's failure during the post-war years comes in their attitude towards linking Heathrow, the world's busiest airport, to London, one of the world's greatest cities. Any private sector entrepreneur with an interest in that part of the railway network would have seen at some point between 1945 and 1995 that the phenomenal growth of Heathrow provided a great transport opportunity. The Great Western mainline into Paddington passed within a couple of miles of Heathrow Airport. Yet at no point during the 50 years of national ownership after 1945 did the nationalised railway industry succeed in proposing and building a fixed rail link from the centre of the airport to the Great Western in order to run trains onward from there to Paddington. Why should this be?

It shows that public monopolists are not creative business people like their private sector counterparts. They lock themselves into a relationship with government, seeing the government as their principal customer and the taxpayer in the case of the railways as their principal source of finance and certainly their source of subsidy as last resort. Their whole habit of mind was to lobby the government for more money to do whatever they wished to do to maintain the existing railway network. They did not look to the fare box and to the opportunities to grow the market for rail travel by making the new links that modern travellers require.

The nationalised industry inherited a very strong railway network in the country geared to the demands of the Victorian and early twentieth century centres of population and industry. The nationalised industry watched as industry and housing estates migrated away from the old railway line of the Victorians towards the new trunk road and motorway network of the latter twentieth century. They did nothing to move with it.

The telecommunications industry was never able to plan a rational network capable of meeting all the sophisticated business demands of the emerging financial services market in London in the 1960's and 1970's. I remember working from an office a few hundred yards from the Bank of England and finding it almost impossible to get a phone line that did not degrade when it was raining, interrupting the data flows to the computers. When I wanted a gas supply to a house three miles outside Oxford I was told by the gas monopolist that he had no statutory requirement to take a pipe that far out of one of Britain's principal cities and therefore had no intention of supplying me. The monopolist dug in around his statutory duties and decided that additional customers were the last thing that he wanted as, on that occasion, he claimed to be 'short of gas'.

A public monopolist puts safety before profits

In both the nationalised transport and energy industries in the UK after 1945, one of the prime arguments used to justify nationalisation and its retention was the argument that only a public monopoly would take safety sufficiently seriously. The Labour left assiduously built up the idea that free enterprise railways would spend too little on safety and kill more passengers. The public monopolists in the gas industry were happy for people to believe that gas is a highly dangerous and volatile fuel. In the private sector, they hinted, there would be more explosions.

The experience of privatisation has been altogether different. Competitive enterprises realise that safety is crucial. They know that if they get a reputation for unsafe conduct it will be extremely difficult to retain their existing customers and all but impossible to win new ones. The airline industry is an extremely competitive business. Competing airlines are constantly looking for ways to reduce their costs under remorseless pressure from each other and from the desire of the travelling passenger to go further for less money. The advent of a whole series of low cost airlines has been very attractive to the public who willingly go on airlines that offer flights at a fraction of the standard fares on the principal carriers. The public do this because they do not believe the low cost carriers will place low cost before their safety. They know that it is a heavily regulated industry but they also know that any sensible airline management is struggling to maintain the highest possible standards of safety. If an airline were to get a reputation for risking safety it would find it very difficult to attract the travelling public and would soon go bankrupt.

It is also the case that in some public enterprises exercising monopoly rights there is a willingness to use safety as a bargaining counter for more money. When the public monopolist has one of his regular bargaining sessions with the government over how much public subsidy should be put into the business or how big a price increase should be permitted, safety often tops the agenda. Safety is said to be the swing factor in allocating the amount of money available. The intention is to put Ministers under pressures, saying that unless more subsidy is made available or unless a fare or price rise is permitted, it would not be possible to spend all the money on technical improvements to safety that the monopolist judges desirable.

During the period of nationalised monopoly control there were all too many crashes on the railways and there were gas explosions and other difficulties in the gas industry. There is no evidence from the post privatisation experience that any of these problems got worse and in some cases they improved. The railway industry in the private sector was required by the incoming Labour government to increase its expenditure on safety. In practice the government concluded that safety expenditure over the many years of nationalisation had been totally inadequate, leaving trains without automatic train warning and protection systems. A spate of incidents where drivers drove trains through red lights led the government and regulator to conclude that there needed to be automatic technological solutions to this problem which the nationalised industry had not been prepared to fit.

Unfortunately, mistakes will be made in both the public and private sectors that will lead to deaths and injuries. There is nothing inherent in free enterprise that makes such errors more likely than in the state sector. Indeed, the way poor safety can lead to a collapse of customer support, and ultimately of the business itself, puts extra pressure on the managers of competitive businesses to take safety seriously. The contrast between the safety record of the US and the USSR space programmes, where the United States performed better, illustrates that relying on the lowest cost bidder for all the equipment on the US space vehicles did not lead to more accidents.

A public monopoly will do a much better job looking after the environment

If we believe in rational planning then it should follow naturally that a public network could produce less damage for the environment than the entrepreneurial spirits of competing companies. If such a public monopolist were able to maximise efficiency, he should be able to reduce the amount of land required for the construction of plant. If an energy producer were able to minimise wasteful fuel burn then he would maximise the cleanliness of his activity. If a public telephone monopolist were able to plan a network to minimise the cable runs he could reduce the number of areas where overhead wires needed to be hung in an unsightly way over telegraph poles.

In practice, once again, we discover the reality is very different from planning theory. The electricity monopoly's decision to concentrate on coal-fired power stations made Britain the dirty man of Europe for many years. The low levels of fuel efficiency combined with the high levels of emissions from the smoking chimneys greatly added to air pollution of several types. Nor did the electricity industry go out of its way to reduce the visual impact of their unsightly plants upon the environment. The decision to build a large coal-fired power station at Didcot in an open valley, visible from miles around, maximised the visual intrusion and damage to the local amenity which could have been reduced by location in a more remote and better concealed coastal location. A coastal location would also have permitted coal to be moved in by ship, a more environmentally friendly method of moving heavy bulk commodities.

The telephone industry, whilst a nationalised monopoly, made little effort to conceal its cables and wires in rural areas, draping unsightly cables over rudimentary telegraph poles in many beautiful villages and countryside settings. The electricity industry went one better, slinging high-tension high voltage cables on massive pylons that marched across some of the most beautiful tracts of the English landscape. When challenged about these environmental outrages, the industry would say that it was too expensive to bury the cables or to conceal them through better design. Many people living under high voltage cables complain about the health impact of the magnetic fields and other forces given off.

The nationalised monopolies often got away with things environmentally that no private sector competing market place would have been allowed to do by the regulators of the day. The close relationship between the nationalised monopolists and the government meant that different rules often applied. The so called 'statutory undertakers' had rights to acquire land, build structures and gain access that would be denied to private sector contractors in different areas. The biggest single mistake of the power industry was the decision to build coal stations that are so dirty. It is very difficult to sustain the argument that public monopolies are good for the environment given this experience. The contrast between the high pollution levels of the communist bloc in the 1980's and the lower pollution levels in Western Europe reinforces this picture.

Public enterprises create equality throughout the country

Creating equal service and treating people fairly is meant to be one of the spin offs from the rational planning that a public monopoly should be able to create. In practice public monopoly does not even create equality of misery when trying to gain access to the services offered.

There are different interpretations of this principle. The postal service was based upon the same charge for any item of mail of similar weight, wherever it was going within the UK. Charging was differentiated by weight and size of item but not by distance travelled. Some claim that it would not be fair to charge people more for their post because they live in a remote Scottish village wishing to send items to southern cities than people in London wishing to send letters to each other. However, when it comes to telephone calls, charging is based upon a combination of the length of the conversation and the distance involved. People pay more for their calls if they live in a remote rural location and wish to talk to a large number of people in more populated centres well away from their home. It is thought sensible to offer them a discount for talking to someone a long way away if they use the less busy times of day. Similarly in the case of the post, customers are offered a discount if they are prepared to put up with later delivery by using second-class mail.

These complicated differential charging systems developed by public monopolists in the communication business illustrate that the principle of equality is not applied universally. The person living in the remote Scottish village will pay far less for housing than someone living in central London. This can be used as a justification for them paying more to ring someone in London than a Londoner ringing a neighbour. Yet it is thought likely that making them pay more for their post would somehow plunge them into poverty, based presumably on the unlikely supposition that they would wish to write to a very large number of people living hundreds of miles away on a regular basis.

The actual patterns of postal communication in recent years are in stark contrast to this egalitarian theory. There has been a sharp decline in the number of individual letters written by people to distant friends and relatives. It is a very rare occurrence these days for most people to write a large number of letters that they wish to send over long distances person to person. There has been a large rise in business to people correspondence where the charging is negotiated between the business concerned and the postal monopoly. If the business is prepared to do part of the Post Office's work for it by delivering the post into a sorting or concentration centre, and if the business is prepared to guarantee certain high volumes, the price is substantially reduced. Public sector monopoly apologists see nothing inegalitarian in the access of big business to discounts not available to the normal customer but would be horrified at any suggestion that charging should be distance related for the domestic user.

Before privatisation, the public enterprise monopoly energy businesses often charged their poorer customers more. They were keen to impose prepayment meters on people who found paying the bills difficult. They used these devices to increase the costs of power they were supplying compared with the more normal arrangements of quarterly billing in arrears. It may have been a rational business decision but it was far from promoting greater equality. Nor did a public monopoly achieve a uniform quality and range of service provision throughout the country. I had to wait more than six months to get a telephone installed when I refurbished a cottage outside Oxford, as the monopolists did not much fancy digging the trench to provide the cable. Nor would the monopolist accept my offer of a higher price for delivering the connection early, as he had a set of standard prices regardless of the complexity of the work. People in remote locations remained disconnected from the telephone and electricity systems for many years under nationalised monopolies. A large number of people were unable to get connected to the main sewerage system provided by the integrated water and waste water disposal monopolies as again the monopolists did not think it worthwhile to make the necessary links.

The public monopoly creates stability of employment and better conditions for employees

Employees in the principal public monopolies were heavily unionised. The trade unions were great advocates of the public monopoly system, believing that this would give their members better pay and conditions and reduce the uncertainties of commercial competition. In practice, things again turned out very differently. If you worked for the public coal, rail or steel monopolies during the years of nationalisation you were very vulnerable to redundancy. Each of these large enterprises, for a variety of reasons, lived through a period of sharp decline in their activities between 1945 and their privatisation. Not all the decline was the result of public monopoly provision, but it is undoubtedly the case that bad planning and bad business decisions by the public monopolist in each of these industries exacerbated the downturn and increased the likelihood of redundancy.

Morale was rarely high in these industries despite having the trade union perceived advantage of public monopoly and rational planning. The industries were strike-torn with frequent resorts to union action or work-to-rule. Those in charge of the public monopolies did not develop new styles of management that enabled the employees to participate more and feel they were co-owners of the business. Often, Parliamentary debates had to be arranged at short notice to discuss why yet more people were losing their jobs or why employees were being treated badly in a nationalised industry, without proper consultation and involvement.

Public enterprises are needed to control natural monopolies

Once the big nationalised networks had been established after 1945 there was a wish to create the impression that they were somehow God-given or natural and could not be disrupted, broken up or made competitive again. Folk memories faded of how competitive railways in the Victorian period had ushered in a phenomenal expansion of railway travel, raising capital to build many new lines. Memories had long since faded of the canal boom when free enterprise had again raised substantial sums in subscription to drive new canals between the bustling commercial centres of industrial revolution Britain. There was an attempt to get people to believe that because canals, railways, the national grid and the water pipes were important national networks, it was somehow God-given that these should be national monopolies.

The strongest defence of the national monopoly line came when the Conservative government tried to privatise the water industry. We were told that God or nature supplied the rainfall and provided the rivers from which water could be extracted. These were a given, which only a public monopoly could properly supervise and control. It would be an outrage, they thundered, for private, profit-making companies to try to exploit what was clearly a natural monopoly. Closer examination showed that the water industry was far from a natural monopoly. In Britain, water was mainly collected and distributed within given water basins. There was very little attempt to create a national network, leapfrogging the principal river valleys of the country. The one main exception, the decision to collect water in reservoirs in mid-Wales and route it to Birmingham by pipe, caused enormous political friction putting people off similar experiments in the future. The nationalised industry recognised the water basin management approach, arguing passionately against the national water grid and saying that using something like the canal network to take water around the country was impossible. The industry remained organised in the form of water boards, later to become water companies, based around a water basin in each case.

The defenders of the monopoly, when challenged on this nature of the industry, shifted their ground to defending the proposition that because water came from the heavens or was routed through the rivers it was somehow wrong for private companies to seek to exploit this. It is quite true that rainfall is God or nature given, depending upon your belief but so is everything else that private industry exploits. The same could be said of stone from quarries, of oil from wells or food from plants. In each of these other cases it has long been accepted that the effort put into collecting, tending, cleaning and packaging should go rewarded and can often best be organised in a private competitive market. What is the difference between the water company collecting the rainfall, cleansing it and routing it through pipes to a customer's house and the oil company drilling for the oil, refining it and routing it to the customer by road tanker? Water is no more a natural monopoly than oil and is best organised, like oil, by competing companies.

Defenders of monopoly in Britain also try to give the impression that somehow water was a scarce resource which needed public monopoly control in the interests of fairness. The water industry under nationalised ownership spent considerable sums of money on advertising to try to persuade people not to use its product. They were very keen to stop people using their product when they most needed it. In summer, when people wished to water their gardens, they often imposed a ban on hosepipes. People were free to use their hosepipes in the wet time of the year in the autumn. In some cases the water literally ran out under nationalised control, giving support to the idea that water was in some way a precious and limited commodity in these rain-strewn islands.

When the industry was privatised it emerged that the nationalised monopoly only succeeded in collecting 3% of the rain falling in Britain and routing it to the customer. It also of course emerged that there is something called the water cycle. Water is not destroyed, merely recycled and reused. If you wish to have more of it you can simply clean it and reuse it more often. As privatisation started to get to grips with the problems of the water industry so water shortages started to reduce. I have not suffered a hosepipe ban in my part of the country ever since the industry was privatised and I look forward to the day when the water industry starts to advertise for people to use its product more rather than less. Shouldn't we be encouraged to shower twice a day rather than being urged, as under nationalisation, to have fewer baths with less water in each?

A public monopoly can give people more provision than the market would otherwise supply

This is perhaps the best case for public monopoly that there is. There are certain goods that people might not wish to buy themselves at all or in large quantities, which can be provided by public monopolies where the government has decided to override the decisions of the market place. The best example of this is the case of defence. In a pure free market world, people would be left to buy the amount of defence they felt they wanted which might be considerably less than the country currently purchases. People might well club together to provide neighbourhood defence against criminal violence and vandalism. They would be less likely to combine in significant numbers to pay for armies capable of invading Afghanistan or policing Bosnia. The decision to create a public monopoly enables the government to marshal the necessary financial and manpower resources it needs by effectively overriding the market and superimposing democratic decisions upon market decisions.

This does not mean however, that to do this the government always has to create a public monopoly. The government, for example, could still have a statutory requirement that every child had to go to school but need not provide all the school places through a public monopoly. The private market would be quite capable of meeting the required standard. Places could still be paid for by the taxpayer. We will examine this in more detail when exposing the disadvantages of public provision.

THE DISADVANTAGES OF PUBLIC MONOPOLIES

Monopolies have many disadvantages. The main ones are that they often overcharge and can deliver a poor service. They rarely seek to innovate and develop new technology as rapidly as a private, competitive market place and frequently suffer from under-investment. There is a temptation to serve the staff and the political masters more than the customers. There is a reluctance to drive out inefficiencies. They usually become extremely bureaucratic. Surprisingly, they can also be bad for employment, as entirely new activities rise up in the competitive market place to supplant them. The monopolist often damages the environment claiming some greater good from what he is doing. There are few natural monopolies, contrary to common opinion, and very often monopolies end up providing the wrong amount of service, sometimes providing too much and often too little.

Overcharging

Many private sector business people are keen to get monopoly or near monopoly power for the very reason that it would enable them to increase their prices to a point where they could make large profits with minimum effort. This is why in most sensible advanced western jurisdictions there are strong anti-monopoly provisions applying to the private sector. Competition law has grown up to prevent direct overcharging and to prevent cartels, mergers and acquisitions which lead to monopoly or near monopoly positions. Price fixing between companies which should compete is illegal and monopoly exploitation by a company which has gained a strong market position, for whatever reason, is also usually condemned.

Public monopolies are past masters at overcharging. Between 1960 and 1975 nationalised industry prices increased by 25% more than the general level of retail prices as measured by the government's retail price index. This trend continued for a few more years until privatisation, deregulation and competition started to make their mark on the former nationalised monopolies. Public enterprise usually managed to combine rapid increases in fares and charges with losses or very small profits. They did this by low productivity and a very high cost base. The answer was always to put up the fare or the price rather than taking action to deal with the underlying cost problem. By the early 1980's, productivity in Britain's nationalised monopolies was well below that of comparable organisations on the Continent, let alone far behind that of a more competitive market place in the United States of America. Overcharging was the natural result of the mistakes made in investment choices and employment levels by the leading public enterprises.

Nationalised monopolies deliver poor service

Poor service to the customer is another way that a nationalised industry combats its very high cost base. Public monopolies also think they are unable to secure enough money from the government to deal with the high cost base and to meet its investment needs. Poor service takes many guises. In some cases it means no service at all, in other cases it means service after enormous delay. The National Health Service refuses to offer certain kinds of treatments and often requires people to wait for eighteen months or two years before getting the operation they need. Without price rationing one ends up with queue rationing.

The water industry, even though it charged its customers direct, often rationed its product and refused many people mains drainage. Substantial numbers of people could get no access to service from British Gas at all. Train travel is rationed at the morning peaks. The inadequate supply means that some people do not try to get on the train and others have to stand, even though they have paid full ticket price for a seat. The nationalised railway often suffered from late trains or from strikes disrupting the service altogether. The London Underground, still a public monopoly, now regularly closes down lines for repair work during busy weeks and is subject to disruption by random industrial action. The nationalised telephone monopoly was unable to offer many of the new services to business that were available in the United States of America in a more competitive market in the 1970's and early 1980's. In these years there was a shortage of main capacity which put the telephone monopoly off trying to extend the range of service.

Public monopolies usually lack the impetus to improve technology rapidly

Sometimes public monopolies do attempt to make a technological leap but often this results in catastrophic failure because their normal mode is to regard the existing technology as sufficient unto the day. The railway industry did move away from coal burning steam trains but made a mess of the alternative technologies it introduced. Some parts of the network use overhead electrical power, some rail electrical systems and some diesel locomotives. It means that there is no benefit from a national network of trains. The type of trains running on the Southern Region, requiring single electrified rail, cannot run on any other part of the network. The faster trains going north on the Great Eastern route require overhead gantries so they are quite unable to run on Southern Region or Western Region. It also means variable standards of service and speed and very different maintenance requirements, negating any possible benefits of scale from owning the whole network.

By the late 1970's the railways in Britain under nationalised ownership became aware that the main constraint on running faster trains on the big inter-city routes, particularly from London to the north, was the large number of bends and curves on the existing track. Out of the two possible solutions to this problem, building a new straighter track or developing trains that could be speed round the bends more safely, the railway decided on the latter. It spent considerable time, money and effort on developing tilting trains in conjunction with the rail engineering industry only to discover, when it wanted to bring them into operation, that they did not work properly. After considerable time, trouble and money they abandoned the idea for the time being.

Britain was left with relatively low speed inter-city trains compared with the bullet trains of Japan or the fast inter-cities of France and Germany. Britain is a very innovative country, with many people capable of thinking up and developing interesting ideas suitable for commercial exploitation. In the post war period United Kingdom designers and engineers made an important contribution to the development of jet engines, the hovercraft, computers and motor vehicles. It is difficult to think of examples of important new technologies developed and pioneered by public monopolies in Britain which, on the whole, have stagnated but have sometimes made large mistakes by trying to leapfrog their technical problems in the wrong way.

Public monopolies tend to under-invest

The traditional supportive analysis of public monopolies in Britain states that there would be nothing wrong with them that more investment money from the government could not put right. If only, the apologists say, the railways had been given more money to spend on new trains and track in the 1970's and 1980's. If only the telecommunications industry had been given more money in the 1970's maybe it could have come up with a better service. We have to ask ourselves why it is that under governments of three different persuasions, Conservative, Labour, and Labour/Liberal coalition since 1945 nationalised industries have always felt under-funded? Why is it that this scarcity of capital afflicts them much more than the private enterprise sector?

Some would say that because every penny the nationalised industries spend on public investment counts against the public expenditure totals for the country as a whole, it imposes an artificial limitation or constraint which does them damage. Because, the argument runs, they are not able to spend as much as they would like on investment, it follows that they must fail in their ventures. One might think that if their capital is limited artificially they would earn very big returns, especially given the phenomenal pricing power they have enjoyed and often used at the expense of the customer. Yet analysis shows that the returns on nationalised industry investment have been disappointing and often non-existent, arguing that to have given them more capital would hardly have improved the situation. It is difficult to escape the conclusion that the nationalised industries, particularly the monopoly ones, were very bad investors and that keeping them short of capital probably spared us yet more horrendous losses along the lines of the tilting trains.

Without market forces and the probing questions of bank managers and stock markets, public monopolies have found it difficult to draw up a proper priority list for investment. It is certainly true that when industries have been privatised they have increased their investment spend quite substantially and raised their returns on capital without increasing prices, usually by changing the type of investment dramatically. The electricity industry turned to entirely different types of power generation. The water industry turned to pipe renewal and improvement, trying at last to tackle the problem of massive water loss that the nationalised industry simply ignored. The railway industry turned to providing new trains and new rail links.

It is undeniably the case that public monopolies have been kept short of investment compared with the amount of money that a freely competitive market place would have supplied. It is also the case that most of the public monopolies, most of the time, showed no felicity in their choice of investment projects. More investment could not be justified given the poor returns and the poor decisions.

Public monopolies serve the politicians and the senior staff more than the customers
In a public monopoly the natural temptation is to look upwards rather than outwards. As so many decisions need the ultimate approval of the politicians and senior management, as the services are so centralised in decision-making and as they are always looking to the government to provide any additional money, it is an understandable reaction. It is a good test of how customer oriented a business is to see the reactions of junior staff if faced with the dilemma of dealing both with the visit of a senior director or politician and with the demands of customers. In most nationalised industries people would not hesitate to defer and to take more seriously the claims of the visiting dignitary than the customer. In a sensible competitive business people would understand that the customers are the life blood of the business and the directors would naturally give way to the customers. In many cases the public monopolies communicated the sense that they felt they had only one customer, the government. As long as they could keep the government on side, whether by being friendly to the government or by offering suitable menaces to it, they felt they would be all right.

Inefficiencies are not driven out: there is no market pressure
In a competitive market, shareholder owned companies are driven to improve or else they die. From the top, the companies' managements are under pressure from the shareholders and their representatives to deliver turnover growth and profits. From the market place the company is under remorseless pressure from customers who are happy to leave and go elsewhere if the service is not good enough, if the price is not right, if they no longer like the business that is serving them. If a competitor finds a better way of doing something, the business has to match it or suffer the consequences.

The public monopoly is not under these direct pressures. Whilst it is theoretically under pressure from the politicians representing the long suffering tax payer, in practice the relationship is often the other way round, with the public monopoly putting pressure on the politicians by blaming any failings of the business upon shortage of money. Similarly, although in theory the customers of a public monopoly could rise up and demand improvement, in practice they usually feel powerless to do so, being in no position to take their business down the road to a different supplier. What happens in practice is that the long-suffering customers, wherever possible, try to find a private sector competitive alternative to the type of good or service being supplied by the public monopoly. In the case of travel they walked away from public enterprise bus and railway companies in their millions, choosing instead to spend money on a private car. In the case of gas, many switched to oil to enjoy the benefits of competitive supply. Public monopoly covers its inefficiencies with real price increases on a sustained basis. It also seeks payment for its inefficiencies from the government, pleading this is an easier route than tackling the underlying inefficiencies themselves.

Public monopolies are bad for jobs

Public monopolies can be bad for jobs. One of the biggest paradoxes in any study of the performance of public monopolies is that they manage to combine low productivity with a propensity to sack a large number of their staff. The reason is simple. Lower productivity induces poor service and high prices, causing people to look elsewhere for a suitable alternative. As a result most of the public monopolies in the post 1945 period presided over sharp declines in their market and their activities. The British steel industry lost comprehensively to foreign competition, which was smarter and cheaper. The British coal industry went through a long period of decline as people turned, where possible, to cheaper and cleaner fuels. The ship building industry lost out to foreign competition, the railway industry lost out to road transport and, although there was growth in telecommunications, the growth was not nearly as fast and as furious as in freer jurisdictions like the United States of America. In the period from 1960 to 1975, British Gas lost 1.4% of its employees every year, British Rail lost 5_% of its workforce every year, British Steel lost 2_%, the electricity industry 1.6%, the Coal Board 1.9% and National Bus 3.4%. This is well ahead of the rate of losses of the manufacturing industry as a whole at 0.7% a year. Of the major public monopolies, only the Post Office telecommunications division showed employment growth. When an industry is sacking 5% of its workforce a year, morale is by definition low and labour relations problematic.

Public monopolies damage the environment

Public monopolies often damage the environment and get away with it. Over the years politicians have been very good at looking the other way when environmental outrages have been caused by public monopoly activities. The public sector railway industry was able to plan and get early permission to put in the Channel Tunnel rail link which, of course, required private capital to actually build. Being a public sector project in its origins, there was nothing like the controversy over the huge swathes of Kentish countryside that would be spoiled by putting in the link that there would have been if the government had proposed a new motorway. The nationalised canal industry similarly found it quite easy to get planning permission to cut a new canal across the countryside from Milton Keynes to Bedford, whilst the energy industries have found it quite easy to get planning permission for large and often dirty installations, frequently built in inappropriate places.   If the nationalised bus industry had taken the environment more seriously it would have made much more rapid strides to replace ageing buses in the vehicle fleet and improve the pollution controls more rapidly than it did. The nationalised monopolies have got away with it because the politicians have not wished to stand up to them on environmental matters.

There are in practice few, if any, natural monopolies

There is no reason why the provision of energy or water, train travel or bus travel should be a monopoly, any more than the provision of food, clothing, shelter and motor vehicle travel should be natural monopolies. If we compare and contrast air travel with rail travel we see what nonsense it is to suppose that train travel is a natural monopoly. The requirements for air travel are much more complex than those for rail travel. Air travel takes place in three dimensions rather than two and it would be disastrous if an aeroplane were held up above an airport for too long, running out of fuel. Despite this, there are different organisations owning and regulating the air space above the airport, the airport runway and taxiways, the ownership and running of the planes and the terminal facilities. Plane travel is delivered by competing operators in a cut-throat market place. It is easier to design a system for the railways allowing choice and competition with fewer safety hazards from doing this than in the case of air travel.

Nor is the water industry a natural monopoly. It is quite possible for people to collect their own rainwater and to purify it themselves. Many people are forced to handle their own dirty water with septic tanks, as they remain unconnected to the main sewer system. Competing water providers could use a common pipe system, as competing oil companies do, to get their oil from the field to nearer the customer.

Electricity generation is another clear example. It is true that it should be more economical to generate power out of very large stations than from small ones. However, it is quite possible for people to generate their own power with a home or standby generator. During the period of public monopoly many businesses felt they needed such a standby facility to combat the danger of interrupted supply owing to strikes and technical malfunctioning of the national system. In a country the size of the United Kingdom, or even of England alone, we are way beyond the point where it would be possible to generate all the power required in a single station. As soon as we accept a pattern of several stations the opportunity arises of having different owners and competing prices.

Public monopolies deliver the wrong amount of service

Public monopolies often deliver the wrong amount of a service. Sometimes a public monopoly delivers too much service, but more often than not it under-delivers, relying on rationing and queues. The worst modern example of this in Britain is the NHS. The service seems to accept the proposition that it should always keep people waiting, in contrast to the much more rapid treatment delivered by something like the American, insurance-backed system. Most observers agree that the Health Service is short of capacity. There is an agreement between many of the providers in the hospitals and many of the patients and commentators that the health service needs more doctors, more nurses and, above all, more beds and operating facilities. The government says it is prepared to make large amounts of extra money available and yet somehow this money fails to deliver the extra facilities that many have decided are necessary. It is the central paradox of public provision. With all the goodwill and with quite a lot of money available, it still remains impossible apparently for such a public service to invest enough and deliver enough to meet the growing demands of people. It has recently emerged that the number of administrators in the NHS now exceeds the number of beds. It shows the infinite capacity of the bureaucratically run system to absorb the money and to recruit staff in areas that do little to service the public better.

Sometimes public monopoly delivers too much service. This was the case with the railways before the Beeching proposals in the 1960's. The nationalised railway was continuing to run a whole series of services to communities that may well have needed them in the Victorian or early twentieth century period, but could no longer fill the carriages and pay the fares. When the decision was made to cut back the rail network, reducing the number of places served by the railways to reflect the changes in the pattern of demand, a shock ran through the nation. The Beeching cuts are remembered some 40 years later and are held out as an example of what should never be done in a public service.

Sensible reflection on what happened would show the inevitability of it. The public enterprise was quite unable to find new ways of using the facilities it had inherited from the thriving private enterprise railway of the late Victorian period. Devoid of ideas to promote all of the existing track and to use it profitably the railway settled on the next most obvious thing to do, a retrenchment of its facilities. Many people recoiled in horror yet, paradoxically, many of these same people are the very ones who had bought cars and no longer wished to use the railway on a regular basis. The railways throughout the second half of the twentieth century supplied too much capacity on certain routes and at less popular times of the day, but were unable to deliver the extra capacity needed on the modern thriving routes, particularly the commuter routes into the principal places of employment.

Chapter three

HOW FREE ENTERPRISE WORKS FOR US

THE ADVANTAGES AND DISADVANTAGES OF A COMPETITIVE MARKET

The list of advantages and disadvantages of a competitive market are the mirror image of those for public monopoly. A free enterprise competitive market is at the opposite end of the spectrum to the monopoly public provision of service. Where the public monopoly puts up with inefficiencies, the private market place drives them out by the clash of inefficient and efficient companies. Where the public monopoly has to make planned decisions about service level and often goes for a mediocre approach, the private market place remorselessly drives up service standards as one company tries to gain the edge over another.

Comparing fifty years of improving cars with railway coaches

One has only to look at the huge improvements made in the quality of private cars over the last fifty years to see the point at work. The clash of the automobile-producing titans has moved us on from a world of relatively slow cars to much faster cars, from a world of relatively unsafe cars to much safer ones for the passengers, from a world where there was limited choice of colour and design to a world of many different varieties. We now regard in-car entertainment, good heating and cooling systems, disk brakes, automatic gearboxes, heated windscreens, wash wipers, and comfortable seats as necessities in most new vehicles where all of these items were luxuries or unobtainable some fifty years ago. This is in stark contrast to the lack of progress until privatisation in the type of rolling stock turning up at the typical commuter station for the daily journey to work by train. In many cases the commuter stock is still the same as it was thirty or forty years ago and the specification of the new rolling stock doesn't bear the same huge improvements in standards of quality that we have seen in the development of the family saloon car.

The competitive market place puts safety at the top of the list where it is important and matters most to customers. The private market place innovates rapidly and usually successfully. Many try innovations but the failures go to the wall quite quickly leaving the winners to serve the customers. It is much easier to kill off a bad idea in a competitive private market place than in a nationalised public monopoly.

Technical progress - the case of computers

The computer industry shows just what huge strides can be made by allowing a multitude of companies to compete one with another. Forty years ago computers scarcely existed. Pioneering efforts had been made in the Second World War. No-one in the 1950's envisaged a world where an individual would have more computing power on his own desk in the office or at home than the British state had at its disposal to crack the German codes at Bletchley Park; all for about £1,000 of outlay. Yet that is what happened over the remarkable development of the computer industry from 1950 to today. Many different systems were tried, many people competed to supply both the hardware and software. Gradually industry standards emerged and the trustbusters in the United States of America had to move in when Microsoft turned out to be one of the big winners in the market place competition. If we compare the huge changes made in computing with the very slow rate of progress in rail transport we can see the impact that a private competitive market place can have on a whole industry.

Free Enterprise delivers plenty of investment

The private market place does not usually run out of money for investment. If the projects are worthwhile or promising they will find the capital. Quite often projects of little or no value also attract investment money for long enough to discover that they are not going to work. The telecommunications industry shows how investment capital suddenly becomes available when an industry is liberated. In the final days of public nationalised ownership the telecommunication system was held up for lack of investment money in Britain. Once some liberalisation and private capital was introduced there was an explosion in investment activity. Indeed, the rapid growth got out of control towards the end of the 1990's with the companies' over expanding capacity leading to price weakness and better service for customers. The private market place is also better at eliminating bad management. There are many ways that management can be changed. Shareholder pressure, take over or merger, board room revolt are all methods used in the private sector to root out managers who have failed or who have been unlucky and replace them with others. In the public sector it is more difficult. Everything is done under a much greater spotlight of public interest and politicians are often reluctant for a variety of reasons to fire nationalised industry chairmen or chief executives as they fear the retaliation through the press that would probably follow any such action. It is all too easy for a disgruntled former chairman or chief executive of a nationalised industry to get a ready audience with the press and public and to blame the government for whatever may have gone wrong under his tenure.

Would you rather travel by free enterprise Apollo or state produced Sputnik?

The competitive market does undoubtedly spend more on promotion and sales. Some will see this as wasteful, others will see it as part of the fun of the market place, offering people a more informed and colourful choice. Companies do go bankrupt and employees can lose their jobs through no fault of their own if the company has backed the wrong technology, offered the wrong good or service, or is simply badly managed. Employees may have to shift from one company to another as one company rises and another falls. The market aims for lowest cost solutions, whereas its critics will say that the lowest cost is not always the best. A good test of whether people really believe this or not can come by comparing the American and the Russian space programmes. The critics of capitalism would point out to the astronaut mounting the podium of a NASA rocket that every one of the many complicated moving parts of the spaceship he was about to enter had been supplied and manufactured by the lowest cost producer. In contrast the Russian cosmonaut mounting the podium knew that every part had been made by a monopoly producer controlled by politicians and a bureaucracy. In practice, as everyone knows, the American space programme was more successful and safer than the Russian one. What the American astronaut knew when mounting the podium was that, whilst every part had been produced by the producer who had offered the lowest cost tender, it had all been rigorously controlled to high quality standards. Each contract was monitored and enforced by people only too aware of the need for safety and success. The Russian system permitted rather more failures as these could be more easily concealed from the Soviet population. The titanic trial of strength between the Soviet planned system and the American free enterprise system ended in triumph for the free enterprise system, delivering the first man on the moon and going on to deliver surveillance and satellite supremacy.

Free enterprise pays you more

Trade unions have always feared and argued that a competitive market place leads to downward pressure on wages and to poorer working conditions for employees than public monopolies. The experience of the second half of the twentieth century belies this view. In the fifty years since the Second World War, people's wages and living standards have made unprecedented gains, with practically every year showing increases in real wages and spending power. No favourable gap opened up between the wages of public sector employees and private sector employees. Indeed, in times of particularly rapid growth the private sector always pushed ahead leaving the public sector to complain that private sector wages had risen too fast and that labour was being moved from the public sector to the private sector in response. In my own part of the world, the hi-tech based Thames Valley economy is seeing consistent pressure in an upwards direction on wages in the private sector making it difficult on a regular basis to recruit and retain teachers, nurses, policemen and other crucial public sector workers.

It is quite true that jobs and wages are at risk in a free enterprise private sector economy if there is a slump or a recession. Fortunately these have been very rare in the last fifty years and of relatively short duration. Public monopolies are not immune to the pressures. When the world goes into slump the public monopoly transport or energy supplier experiences a similar reduction in demand to that experienced in the free enterprise sector. It is not immune to downward pressures on employment and wages

IS MARKET PRICING OR TAX PAYMENT A BETTER SYSTEM?

Socialism is an ideal which works better in dreams than in reality. To the socialist mind, provision free at the point of use is superior to making people pay for what they enjoy and consume. Modern socialists have withdrawn from arguing the case in many areas, but their arguments retain a family resemblance to their more thoroughgoing forebears when they argue the case for free access to parks, gardens, other peoples' land, to museums, libraries and art galleries. Socialists believe that it is good for people to walk in parks or visit art galleries, but they so lack faith in human nature that they fear if people have to pay to do these things they are unlikely to do so in sufficient numbers. Far better then, they argue, to make it possible for all regardless of income to walk in the park or view the Picassos by the taxpayer paying for the provision of the park or art gallery and the customer getting in free.

There are obvious advantages for the user of the service. If you wish to visit a popular art gallery you avoid the need to queue to buy a ticket, although given free pricing you are likely to have to queue to see the exhibits themselves. The 'waste' of selling tickets to people and supervising their payment is also removed. Poor and rich alike have equal access to the facilities. Their access to the exhibition or to the gardens is dependent only upon the time of their arrival and their place in the queue.

The advantages of free at the point of use

There are four principal advantages put forward for public provision free at the point of use. The first is that the poor get equal access to the service, meaning that people on low incomes have access to health care or to art exhibitions and public parks when they might not be able to afford the private sector equivalent.

The second argument is an egalitarian one. The rich have more restricted access, unable to buy their way into privileged use or access. A rich person cannot arrive at an NHS hospital and say that they want the NHS treatment on a preferential basis because they are prepared to pay. They would have to go to a private hospital down the road instead if their money was to count. Similarly the rich cannot say that they would like to have a private party in Regents Park and to keep everyone else out for its duration as it is simply impossible to buy Regents Park for the day.

The third argument is that by removing the need to price and charge you should be able to simplify and reduce the cost of the service whilst enabling the staff to concentrate on more important matters. Socialists were very exercised when the move to a so called internal market in the Health Service created the need for managers to be aware of the costs and prices of service supplied between different parts of the NHS itself. A long campaign was waged to try and get internal pricing out of the NHS on the grounds that these resources could then be spent in better ways.

The fourth argument is paternal. It is that the free provision of services will ensure that people enjoy the services they ought to enjoy but would not choose to buy for themselves. Some people might think it worthwhile going to see the Constables in the National Gallery if there was no charge for doing so but could think of better ways of spending their money if they had to pay an entrance fee. Socialists are keen, apparently, for more people to spend their time gazing at Constables and less time watching football matches or attending pop concerts where the principle of high charges has been well established for a long time.

Why free at the point of use is not always a good idea

Each of these propositions is questionable. The poor do not always get access to the service as imagined. A lot of people do not go to see the Constables or the Turners even though they are free because they do not know about it, or they do not value the idea, or do not think it would be a good way to spend their time. Nor is the access itself free. For, whilst the taxpayer takes care of the costs of running the art gallery, the individual has to pay his own money in order to get the family there and back. He may have to spend more highly for a meal away from home than if he stayed in his own place. Similarly, whilst health care is largely free at the point of use, the individual may end up with a bill for a prescription following a visit to the doctor and will have to make his or her own arrangements for transport unless the condition is an emergency. Because the service is often rationed people on low incomes may well not get the service they require. In my constituency the shortage of health care is now quite acute. As a result many people, some on quite modest incomes, decide they will pay to overcome the problem of the queue. Unless the public sector is prepared to close down every private sector alternative it will always be possible, in a free society, for people to find ways round the queue caused by poor public provision free at the point of use. The poor are the ones with fewest options, left waiting in the queue as the health service grapples with too much demand and too little ability to supply the necessary treatment.

By the same token the rich do not lose all their privileges. Directors of art galleries and exhibitions always want more money than the state can provide. They push their freedoms to the limits, often closing the museum or art gallery to the general public and letting it out for private functions in order to increase their income. They are also quite keen on setting up separate art exhibitions within the gallery for which they can impose charges despite the general rule in favour of free admission. Whilst the rich cannot buy Regents Park for the afternoon, people can use political influence to take over free public facilities for special uses and then effectively close them off to the public in the name of security. The closer one gets to a socialist planned system with free services at the point of use, the more one sees political and bureaucratic influence being used to replace money as a means of allocating to the powerful a bigger share of the enjoyment. In communist societies it is not what you earn but who you know that opens doors. I cannot say I find that system preferable to one where people do respond to the offer of money to carry out a service. It is possible for people with good connections to get better and faster service from British nationalised services.

The argument that free provision saves a lot of expenditure on internal pricing and costing is superficially attractive. No sensible person likes more money to be spent on bureaucracy and paperwork than is strictly necessary. However, experience with the NHS is disappointing. The Labour government came in and claimed to have abolished the internal market and much of the paperwork that went with it. Five years on and we have more administrators and more paperwork despite these changes. Planned bureaucratic systems have an infinite capacity to expand the amount of bureaucracy they need, with or without internal pricing.

Nor does making a service available free at the point of use guarantee that people will want to use it. It is a noble idea that the free provision of art galleries and libraries would turn us into a nation of fine art lovers and well-read people. Experience shows that there are still many who would rather spend their time differently from that of the highbrow socialist tempting them with public bribes to visit a library or a museum. For people to get what they want requires good information. Private sector markets are better at presenting their offers to people through the colour and clash of advertising than the public sector. The public sector has to be more careful about how much it spends on self-promotion and runs the risk of not getting its message home. Many of us are unhappy with the idea of public sector arbiters of our tastes. Who is to say that it is better to spend one's Saturday afternoon gazing fondly at the Turners than to spend the same afternoon drinking beer or attending a football match?

At the beginning of the twentieth century it was commonly argued that most people were not up to owning their own homes. Patronising political and community leaders argued that people on low incomes would not be able to afford to mend the roof or maintain the property. They felt it was much better for a landlord to organise it for them and to collect the rent on a regular basis. How wrong they were. The long march of every man to become a homeowner in Britain has coincided with a huge improvement in the standards of housing and house maintenance. Most owners take a great pride in their property and put to shame institutional landlords in many cases. It is not always right for politicians to decide what is good for people. People are usually better judges for themselves.

In a free service, queues replace price for rationing. It is difficult to buy more or extra and there is a limited list mentality. The take it or leave it service attitude tells people what is good for them and will offer them nothing else. As a result people often do not like it and regularly do not value it.

The advantages of market pricing

Market pricing, in contrast, keeps a sharpness in the competitive business which is usually good for the customer. People can make their own choice of priorities by deciding what they wish to spend more or less of their money on. It gives people something to strive for. Why should people work hard if they cannot earn more money and spend it on things that they want? I remember being fascinated on early visits to Eastern European countries at the time that communism collapsed. People in Romania asked me why people worked so hard in my country. I explained that people worked hard in many cases, working overtime or seeking better performance because they wished to be paid more. But why, they asked, did they wish to be paid more? I explained that people wanted to be paid more because there were many goods and services on offer in the market place that they wished to enjoy. It was when I visited Romanian shops that I understood their incomprehension. Under the communist regime the shops had very little on offer. You could earn more money but there was nothing to spend it on. Your life was completely regulated and, if you earned more than you could spend on the limited range of goods available at the end of the queues, all you could do was lend it back to the state, which had the power to enhance or destroy your savings as it planned and controlled everything. It was the old joke in Eastern Europe that people pretended to work and the state pretended to pay them. There was mutual suspicion on both sides with the public aware of the state's inability to deliver the goods and services they wanted and the state aware of the reluctance of people to work hard.

In a free enterprise system you get exactly the right amount of supply for the demand at the clearing price in the market. There is no need for physical rationing and queues if the price system is allowed to work properly. If too many people want to go to see the Constables so that there are crowds and queues then a simple adjustment of the price will sort the problem out. If too many people turn up for the aeroplane flight and there are not enough seats available, the airline merely has to name an amount of money they will give to anyone volunteering to go on a later flight. Everyone is happy, with those who want to travel on time travelling on time and those who would like some extra money prepared to take that in return for a ticket on a later flight. In free enterprise societies there are not usually problems with empty shelves and queues at supermarkets. In communist Eastern Europe it could take all day to shop for the things needed for a dinner party if you could find them at all, given the empty shelves and the long queues. Parallel market places in a free enterprise society create something for everyone. Because people are exercising their own choice based on the purchasing power their income gives them, they can turn to a whole variety of styles and standards of service and good on offer.

Free enterprise societies have been extremely good at constantly raising the living standards of the people who live in them. The luxuries of the rich in one generation become commonly available in the next and become the necessities of all in the third generation. In the early twentieth century only the rich could own a car. These had become quite commonplace by the middle twentieth century and necessities for most as the century drew to a close. TV's were for the rich in the 1930's and 1940's but are now owned by practically everybody in the country some sixty years later. It was a rare home that had a fridge in the 1950's, it is a rare home which does not have one in 2002. Competitive industry has brought an ever-wider array of labour saving devices, comforts, entertainments and luxuries to the rooms and kitchen tables of the nation.

THE DISADVANTAGES OF COMPETITIVE MARKETS

It is said that competitive markets also bring with them considerable disadvantages:

Some cannot compete

The first often identified is that people can often be too old, ill or incapacitated to work and therefore have no source of income. Such people clearly need help in order to survive in a price driven market economy. In more traditional market economies they receive their help through a combination of informal networks. Most commonly other family members decide to take care of the young, the old and the incapacitated. Nearly everywhere it is accepted that parents should pay for and look after their children wherever possible. In many traditional societies it is also accepted that the working generation should look after the retired generation and often agreed that where a family member is sick or incapacitated, they should be given free board and lodging.

In more advanced capitalist economies democratic societies have usually decided to levy taxes upon the working generation to make provision for those with no such source of income. Most of us willingly pay taxes to transfer money to those who cannot work through incapacity or sickness. Increasingly old age is taken care of by proper savings plans during the working years, augmented by a state pension scheme. It would also be possible to take care of the problem of sickness or incapacity for those who come to it after a period in employment by similar insurance provision. In some advanced western societies an element of insurance is included in the policy mix.

There are too many inequalities
The second big disadvantage of the market economy, especially to those who value equality more than prosperity, is that it does produce big disparities in incomes. If you compare the wages of a first rank, Premier League football team player with the wages of the person who made his shirt the gap is startling. £20,000 per year would be a good rate of pay for a football shirt maker whereas £20,000 per week would not be uncommon for a first rank football player. The reason for the big disparity is obvious. People will pay large sums of money to go in considerable numbers to view the performances of a few highly qualified and highly professional footballers. It would not be possible to take a man out of a shirt factory, train him for a week and get him to achieve the level of performance and play that the best players regularly deliver. Conversely, it would be possible to take most people out of whatever they are doing, train them for a week and expect them to perform perfectly adequately in the shirt factory. If people tire of football and the gate and television money reduces, then the footballers wages will contract. They are able to earn a superior rate while their sport is popular and they are successful.

Nonetheless, most western societies think the large disparities in income between the highest paid and the lowest paid are unacceptable. As a result progressive income taxes are levied on those earning the very large sums of money and redistributed in part to those on low incomes, through the benefit system. What sometimes gets forgotten in the criticism of income inequalities is that market systems generate a much higher average level of income than planned or socialist societies. Indeed, in many cases the lowest incomes in the competitive market place of a western capitalist society are above the average incomes achieved in planned communities. After forty years of the experiment with socialism in Eastern Europe and mixed free enterprise and state planning in

Western Europe, the decisive victory of the west showed through. As a result people in the planned societies overturned their governments and adopted the western model.

Are markets wasteful?

Market pricing, it is said, is also wasteful in ways we have already examined. The moneyless economy of the communist dream turned out to be a practical nightmare. The diseconomies created by the absence of price more than overwhelmed the advantages of not having to pay for the pricing system itself.

THE ARGUMENTS FOR AND AGAINST PUBLIC PROVISION

The arguments for and against public provision contain elements of the arguments for and against providing service free at the point of use and elements of the arguments about whether monopoly or competition is better. Those in favour of public provision argue it is safer, fairer, provides central planning and sensible decisions, it is rational, it is easier to use and live with and benefits from government control and interest in standards. The opponents dislike the take it or leave it attitude, the secrecy, the practical lack of safety, the unequal misery, the inefficiencies, the lack of incentive and the lack of ownership. There are a few arguments specifically related to whether something should be publicly or privately provided in addition to the cut and thrust of the debate about monopoly and market pricing.

Is there a superior public sector ethos?

The main argument put forward by proponents of public provision is that the public ethos is much better than the private, competitive, profit-making spirit. They draw a contrast between people in the public sector whom they see as entirely motivated by the public good (rationally deciding in favour of the best for the most) with the selfish decision making of private entrepreneurs, out to maximise their profits whatever the impact they may have upon the society around them. The caricature lives long and goes deep in socialist literature of the cigar-smoking, fat, overpaid entrepreneur who does not care a damn about the environment, the community, the society or the feelings of people around him and who is prepared to cut any costs and cut any corner in order to make a profit. In the name of dealing with him socialist thinkers demand an ever-bigger array of regulation, interference, and control over the private competing sector. They want the state to take care of the safety, fairness, central standards and justice issues which they think are naturally taken care of in the case of public provision.

So we must ask is it true that in the public sector there is this totally different ethos, the spirit of public service, which means much better results than the selfish competitive spirit in the private sector? It is certainly the case that it is possible to find highly dedicated, hard-working, talented civil servants and public officials who are motivated by the best of considerations and who dedicate their lives to the public service in the true sense. But it is also true that if you look at the system as a whole the public sector ethos is far from elevating and high-minded. Rates of absenteeism and sickness in the public service are always on average much higher than equivalent rates of sickness and absenteeism in the private sector. This reflects the spirit amongst some in the public services that it is the employees' entitlement to have a certain number of days off each year for sickness whether they are truly sick or not. It reflects the lack of commitment on average to the task in hand, with heavily unionised work forces usually thinking about the hours and conditions of work and the things that directly relate to their own conditions of employment more than to the public they serve. Public services are rarely available on Sundays and holidays as public service employees think it is important they have the day off. In a rational world the public services would be more adequately supplied and provided at the weekends and during holiday periods when more of the public were in a position to enjoy them. In all too many local communities libraries are shut in the evenings or on public holidays when people with jobs would be able to spend some time choosing books or consulting the reference works. Over Christmas, the New Year and at Easter there are no refuse collections from local councils in most parts of the country yet we still get a daily paper and fresh bread.

How much does the public sector care?
There is throughout the public sector inefficiency verging on carelessness towards the ultimate users of the service. For example, when the national or local highways agencies decide that they need to resurface, mend or improve a road they close it in whole or part for as long as it takes to do the work. This usually entails closing the road, day in day out, including at the busiest times of the working day. Can one really believe that a private sector company would behave like this? We certainly do not see the closure of the main runway at Heathrow during the busiest revenue earning periods. Resurfacing work is carried out overnight during the hours when no flights are permitted.

Taxation – the public sector's Achilles heel

Perhaps the worst feature of public provision is the requirement that it imposes on local and national government to raise money in taxation. The myth grows up that something like the Health Service is free. It is important to always use the phrase 'free at the point of use' to remind people that it is far from free. Every individual in the country now pays an average £1000 in taxes each year for the NHS: that is £4000 for the average family. Every time you buy a gallon of petrol and pay 80% tax on it, every time you buy a good in the shop with VAT at 17.5%, every time you pay income tax or national insurance, you are making a contribution to the substantial cost of the NHS. A local council has to send every household a regular council tax bill. The British Broadcasting Corporation imposes a poll tax called the Licence Fee. Every tax leads to complications and pain for the people filling in the forms and making the payments. It is the answer to those who say that it is such a freedom not to have to pay for the service when you use it. It is probably more time consuming and complicated to pay for your health care through income tax and national insurance than to pay at the point of use when you need it. For many people it is considerably dearer to have to pay through the tax system: it is only those who need a lot of health care over their lives who are net winners from the redistribution. Their needs could be looked after through other systems of insurance.

How free is public information?

The public sector ethos is meant to be open, democratic and accountable. Part of the cost of public service provision is the need to have parliaments and councils with all their attendant officials and advisers as well as elected representatives to try to keep the public informed and to keep the service providers up to the mark. Despite the apparent belief in openness and democratic debate to expose the advantages and disadvantages of each public service, there is in practice often a culture of secrecy at the heart of government and the public monopolies themselves. The private sector usually has to be open with its information as part of its attempt to keep it in the market place. For example, investment managers have to be free with their information about how well or badly their funds have done, permitting comparison over time and between different management groups. Any investment manager who refused to make this information available would soon be exposed by the press, the actuaries and the other people involved in performance measurement and analysis. Conversely, until recently it has been impossible to get any performance figures about health care in Britain. When going into a hospital or visiting a doctor it has been impossible to get comparative information on doctors' experience and success rates. The increasing number of sophisticated consumers want to be as well-informed about their public services as they are about their private ones. In some cases secrecy is gradually being blown away, in other cases it remains as an enveloping blanket.

Blame the lack of money for any mistake

Another part of the public sector ethos is to ensure that whenever something goes wrong the most commonly blamed culprit is lack of money or political support. Why are the hospitals dirty? Because they do not have enough money to spend on cleaning. Why do nationalised trains get driven through red lights and crash? Because they do not have enough money to spend on putting in train warning systems to override the driver. Why weren't there enough phone lines in the country in the 1970's? Because the government did not make enough money available to put in the necessary capacity. The easy thing to do is to blame the government and the easy excuse is to say that not enough money was made available. It is very rare to find a public sector manager coming out into the open and admitting that the reason the train crashed was because the driver made a huge mistake, or the reason the hospital was dirty is because the people paid to do the job of cleaning it were not properly supervised. In the private sector when such a problem came to light people would be sacked and action would be taken. In the public sector it is normally the excuse for a further public debate. In bad cases it leads to the writing of a report with lots of recommendations that entail the expenditure of much more money and then a further discussion about how much more money can be made available.

Post-code prescribing and catchment area school results

The public sector ethos is meant to create justice and fairness around the country. Yet, as we have seen, unequal misery is rife at the hands of the public services in Britain. Councils around the country deliver very different standards of education town by town, district by district. Although the poorly performing ones nearly always argue that they need more money in order to improve the service, there is if anything a perverse correlation between low spending and high achievement. This has caused some embarrassment amongst the public sector proponents who would clearly prefer to see a very simple correlation between more money being spent and results getting better. They have been forced into a secondary explanation, arguing that the education authorities that spend least are in counties, cities and districts where the children are most amenable to being taught. Conversely the boroughs and counties that spend most are in areas where apparently the children are less well equipped to learn and less keen to do so. The concept of social inequality has been introduced as a rather patronising way to get out of the difficulty of the lack of results amongst the high spending authorities. Under this theory children from broken homes are more likely to do badly than children from loving homes, children from rich families are more likely to do well than children from poor families and children from educated families are more likely to do well than children from uneducated families.

We should not let this assumption go without challenge. It is very divisive and very patronising. It is certainly not universally true. There are many examples of children from rich family backgrounds who have suffered from parental neglect. Buying the child his own computer game and his own television for the bedroom so that you have to spend less time with him is not necessarily a recipe for a happy child or a better educated one. The loving but poor background, where the parents take a direct daily interest in the child and his or her progress, may be more supportive. Similarly, the absence of books and learning at home does not mean that the child will be against them away from home. What do we have public libraries for if they are not for children from homes without books to go to look up what they want to know? I used public libraries in this way coming from a home with very few books. Conversely, having parents at home with lots of books and a big education behind them may put the child off, making the child feel he or she can never catch up and maybe its better to rebel and do something different. Perhaps we should ask ourselves whether one of the big differences between the low cost schools and the high cost schools is not so much the children as the board of governors and the teachers. I have been very struck by the different expectations of children in different schools in different areas, which seem to matter more than the amount of money actually spent or even the number of teachers available.

The theory that more money will produce better results is directly linked to the theory that more teachers are always better than fewer teachers. This too should not go without question. Some of the countries with the highest educational standards in the world have the highest average class sizes. They achieve these good results and deal with this apparent problem of too few teachers by adapting their teaching techniques to whole class teaching and ensuring that lessons taught are of a very high quality. If the teaching is good enough, it makes sense for more children to hear the lesson. The best professors and teachers attract audiences that can be worldwide. With modern technology we can deliver the best professors and lecturers into the schools and homes of every child. The difficulty in Britain has arisen with child centred, play based systems of learning in the lower age range. Students at secondary school often find it difficult to catch up as they often arrive without the basic skills in English and mathematics that they need to make sense of the secondary curriculum. Having extra adult helpers in the classroom may not make up the difference.

There is no substitute for the successful inculcation of basic language and mathematics in the early years and for teachers in secondary schools who have a love of learning and a passion for their subject and communicate it to the pupils.

We have seen how some people believe that free provision of something like roads makes their use much easier and is a great advantage, part of the public sector ethos. Yet even here, where the absence of the toll does make it easier to use the road, the public sector manages to find a whole series of additional restrictions or requirements that more than offsets the absence of the tollbooth. Most public interventions on the highways are designed to make the journey more difficult rather than easier. The modern fashion is to restrict road space in a variety of ways. Faced with an inadequate road network with insufficient capacity, the public sector merrily goes about its way of imposing more traffic lights, more chicanes, more bumps, more humps, more road narrowing and an ever greater range of warning or mandatory signs by the road side. When the motorist also takes into account the amount of time and effort he has to put in to licensing his vehicle and licensing himself he could be forgiven for thinking that the public provision has not produced a superior answer to paying a toll to a private company for use of a relatively unencumbered highway.

Which serves you better - public monopoly or private enterprise?
The public sector in Britain had thirty-five golden years after the end of the Second World War until the beginning of the Thatcher revolution in the 1980's. This was a good long period to test out the thesis that public provision was always superior to private, that monopoly produced better planned results than competition and service delivered free at the point of use was fairer and better than

service paid for directly. The results of this long period of experiment were deeply disappointing. Most of the benefits that the planners confidently predicted failed to materialise. In many cases the publicly provided monopoly service, especially free at the point of use, delivered less and was less fair than a competitive market where people made their own choices and paid for their own goods.

If we compare the astonishing improvement in holidays which people experienced between 1945 and today with the lack of progress made in health care the comparison is quite startling. Imagine what it would be like if in 1945 the then government had decided on a national holiday service. They could have argued powerfully that all too few people could afford a decent holiday. They could have said that people would lead happier, longer and healthier lives if only they could have a week's holiday by the seaside every year in order to relax and enjoy themselves. They would have taken into public control the bus and coach and train companies to take people to their holiday destinations. They would have taken into control the hotels by the English seaside and they would have begun allocating weeks by the sea to every citizen in the country. The holidays would be provided free at the point of use, but of course taxes would have to be a bit higher in order to meet the phenomenal costs of giving everybody a week's holiday.

The government would have accepted the standards of the day for working class relaxation and entertainment. They would have accepted that people should travel to and from their holiday break by train or bus. They would have accepted that people should enjoy hostel type accommodation, with men and women segregated and sharing hostel dormitory space. They would have accepted that people should get one week's break rather than two and accepted that a range of seaside type entertainment should be provided as part of the standard package.

Fifty years on, much of this structure would still be in place. The system would be creaking under the weight of numbers and its own success. People might have to wait more than a year to get the destination of their choice. Many people would want a week in Bournemouth in August but how many volunteers would there be for a week in Skegness in November? There would be long queues for the popular breaks and attempts by people to avoid the unpopular ones. People would begin to complain about the long queues and delays, the inability to get the holiday of their choice when and where they wanted it and the standards of hostel accommodation at the seaside resorts. People might start complaining that they wanted something more than donkey rides on the beach and Punch and Judy shows. These would begin to look quite dated in the age of the video and the computer game. The system would be under great strain, with difficulties in making the necessary bookings both of the train ride and of the holiday destination hostel. Some would use political and bureaucratic leverage to try and queue jump, others would accept with resignation the delay and wait patiently, while others would decide it was not worth it and drop out of having a holiday altogether.

The reader may think this all sounds rather far fetched, yet when you look at what happened to our health service as a result of having a nationalised monopoly throughout the post-war period you can see obvious parallels. Does anyone seriously believe that if we had a private health service in the post-war period people would still be going into communal hostel type wards and having to accept that they shared their bedroom with ten or twenty other people? Do you really believe if we had a private sector hospital service that going into hospital would mean cutting yourself off from your own colour television, your own computer link and your own phone system? In many a hospital today there is a communal television showing only one of four channels and a communal phone at the end of the ward if you are lucky. Does anyone believe if we had a private system that people would accept they had to wait eighteen months or two years to get in for treatment, having had to wait perhaps six months to find out whether they needed treatment in the first place? If we had had private care would we not have a much wider range of treatments including alternative therapies and remedies? If we compare the enormous strides made in providing affordable holidays to people at places and times of their choice with the changes to our Health Service over the post-war period, the comparison is far from flattering to the publicly provided monopoly. Indeed, the contrast is rather like the contrast between the improvements and enormous increase in standards recorded by the largely free-enterprise west in the post-war period and the lack of progress, the queues, the rationing and the difficulties encountered in providing goods and services in the fully state provided and planned Eastern European territories.

There are good theoretical reasons why competition is always superior to monopoly, and why private provision is usually superior to public. There are more debates over whether it is better always to impose an economic price at the point of use and offer those with low or no incomes suitable income top ups through state redistribution or whether some of that redistribution should be achieved through free goods at the point of use. It is much easier in politics to defend the proposition that the museum should be free or the park should have open access. Even here analysis of the underlying truth shows that where prices are charged, people have more control over their lives and more control over the quality and range of service offered.

There is no particular reason why proponents of free enterprise should feel particularly defensive about the problems of poverty and inequality of income. Socialist systems encourage the greater poverty by the greater number and still allow considerable inequalities, although these are usually achieved by gaining extra political leverage rather than having more spending power. In free enterprise societies, the politicians should sit in the same traffic jam as the people they are taxing to pay their wages. In communist systems where there were far fewer traffic jams because there were far fewer cars the political leadership usually reserved a special lane for themselves so that their limos would never be delayed. In the Soviet system the political leadership were keen to have separate schools for their own children, modelled more on the lines of a British public school, and ensured that there were special shops for themselves and other members of the ruling party which had rather more goods in them than those open to the general public.

Too much public provision means a much higher burden of taxation. Whether the service is free or not, the public sector nearly always requires far more money to be provided by the taxpayer than under the alternative arrangements. High taxes lead to black markets and can lead to capital, ideas and people fleeing the country or avoiding the country as they seek more benign climates elsewhere to ply their trades.

If a country wishes to offer more ownership, a higher standard of living and better services to its public, it needs to make the journey from monopoly to competition, from public provision to private and from free at the point of use to paying in as many areas as possible. As Britain has shown, when this journey is made it can produce astonishingly favourable results.

Chapter four

GOING PLACES

Public or private?

IN BRITAIN IT HAS LONG BEEN a political sport to debate whether a service should be publicly or privately owned and delivered. It may not amount to a great tradition but it has been heated and central to the democratic contest. Between 1945 and 1951 much was nationalised. The general view at that time favoured state planning, believing it would be infinitely superior to competing private businesses. Coal miners queued up to see their industry nationalised in the belief that it would secure their jobs and create better and safer conditions of employment. The railways, buses and freight transport were brought into public ownership, a nationalised health service was set up by the state. State and municipal education was expanded and even the steel industry was seen as a suitable target for nationalisation. Wartime mobilisation entailed taking over the commanding heights of the economy, and subjecting everything to government planning as politicians understandably placed war demands above others. The first post war government was Labour, with many enthusiasts for rational state planning. They decided not to let go.

There were those at the time who objected, especially to the nationalisation of trading enterprises. The Conservative opposition opposed many of the business nationalisation measures but decided, on forming the government from 1951 onwards, to accept much of the settlement. There were changes at the edges. The Conservatives did not agree with steel nationalisation and broke up the large nationalised transport empire. However, they decided to keep the main transport elements in public ownership, especially the railways.

Privatisation – a false dawn

By 1970 the election of a new Conservative government under Edward Heath brought new thinking. The Selsden Park Conference, prior to the 1970 election, pointed the Conservative party in the direction of trusting the market place more and the state rather less. There were high hopes amongst liberal minded Conservatives that at last there might be a government prepared to challenge the idea that a nationalised monopoly was the best way of delivering public service. From1970 to 1974 the government did not have the political will or strength to do anything about reversing the larger nationalisations. Indeed, financial problems facing several private sector organisations including Rolls Royce and British Leyland, the leading British car manufacturer, forced the government in the other direction. Panicking about the possible loss of jobs the government decided on a course of subsidy and investment in private sector companies and industries that had fallen on hard times.

Labour-Liberal government in the 1970's - subsidy and industrial decline

The consensus policy of allowing industrial conglomeration and offering subsidy, support and intervention in the commanding heights of the economy dominated throughout the 1970's. The Labour and Labour-Liberal governments under Harold Wilson and Jim Callaghan, between 1974 and 1979, carried on where Edward Heath left off. They felt they were creatures of circumstance, with debts to the trade unions. It was common wisdom that the way to protect jobs and stave off financial disaster was for the government to take a stake, offer a subsidy, or intervene through lunchtime directives with Ministers in private conversations with company directors. Wedgwood-Benn in the Labour Cabinet wished to go one further and enter into a whole series of planning agreements and back door nationalisations with leading private sector companies. He was largely thwarted by more timid colleagues but the general atmosphere was in Benn's direction. Many people felt that if government subsidy, intervention and monopoly had not delivered the goods so far, the answer was more of it rather than less of it.

A decisive change occurred in the intellectual climate during the course of the 1970's. It was a heady time for those of us who strongly believed that free markets and enterprise would deliver greater prosperity than state control. Sir Keith Joseph set out the general case for enterprise and markets in a series of important speeches and lectures. I wrote fast and furiously about how public enterprises could be split up and returned to the private sector in whole or part. There was a ready audience for such ideas in the form of the new leader of the Conservative Party, Margaret Thatcher. In the 1970's she was cautious about commitments, fearing that the intellectual climate had not moved on sufficiently and worrying about the practicalities of how these things could be achieved. She had been a member of Edward Heath's government. She remembered only too well that between 1971 and 1973 all that had been achieved was hiving off a few BOAC routes to private sector British Caledonian, the sale of the Thomas Cook travel agency and the denationalisation of the Carlisle State Breweries. The impact of this had been more than offset by taking Rolls Royce into public ownership when the company went bankrupt and by the growing government involvement in the British motor industry.

The Thatcher government

Margaret Thatcher's government, from 1979 onwards, began very slowly to shift the balance. The Labour government in 1976, following a financial crisis, was forced into selling some shares in British Petroleum. The Conservatives sold an additional 5%, taking the government's stake down to 46% from the 51% control they had inherited. The National Enterprise Board, a body set up to take stakes in private sector companies and intervene generally in the market place was a particular bête noire of pro-enterprise Conservatives like myself. With Michael Grylls MP, I published a pamphlet on how it should be broken up and closed down. The government was very nervous but in the early days did persuade the NEB's British Technology Group to sell Fairey the engineering company and to place the holding in Ferranti.

These timid beginnings did not bring the house down. Those who were very afraid that the Conservative government was moving too quickly began to lose the argument. In 1981 the government sold British Aerospace and Cable & Wireless, two important businesses. In the balance of the first Thatcher administration the government sold Amersham International, an important technology business, BritOil, Associated British Ports and sold the National Freight Corporation to its employees.

After the 1983 election I was invited into Downing Street to offer advice on privatisation. Reviewing the progress so far my conclusion was that the programme had been useful but was going to have only a marginal impact on the British economy. The early sales had showed that it was a technically and politically feasible process. I urged the Prime Minister to scale the programme up massively. I argued that the first big target for the privatisation programme should be British Telecommunications.

Telecommunications – the first large privatisation and liberalisation

The City was surprisingly reluctant. Many in the City felt that a share issue on the scale of British Telecom's would be impossible. It would be several orders of magnitude larger than anything attempted so far: at that point the largest issue had been the sale of

BP shares as the government reduced its holding. The City thought it might be better to launch some BT Bonds, offering a kind of private sector finance for a state-owned enterprise. The Treasury and the Prime Minister's office were agreed that this would not represent a proper transfer of risk to the private sector and was simply a more expensive way of financing British Telecom's investment programme.

The decision to press ahead with the sale of British Telecom was a decisive moment not just for the British programme but also for privatisation worldwide. Given the reluctance of the City it was important to find other avenues for selling shares. City institutions said there would be too many shares on offer for their appetite. As a result it was decided that we needed to appeal more generally to the public, offering them access to share purchasing for the first time in many cases and offering it direct through newspaper advertisements and postal campaigns. We also decided that we would allow foreign investors to participate in the issue. The scheme I drew up set out to create artificial scarcity amidst plenty. All we had to do was to make it difficult for investment managers in the City to have a similar percentage of BT shares in their portfolio to the percentage that BT would represent of the UK Stock Market as a whole. We brought in new players to buy shares from amongst the general public and from overseas to squeeze the institutions.

The tripartite model for launching share issues in Britain was extremely successful. Indeed most of the political difficulties that arose, arose because the process was so successful, leading to institutional buyers rushing into the market after the share sale had been completed, desperate to increase their holdings and driving the stock prices higher. Opposition turned from suggesting the whole thing would be a flop to arguing that some of the shares had been 'given away', sold too cheaply. The approach of offering shares in the mass market to the wider public was picked up and developed in many other countries overseas as privatisation spread from its narrow British base to become a worldwide phenomenon.

The progress of British Telecom became much more important in other ways. Whilst the transfer of ownership from the state to the private sector was seen as the crucial change, in practice far more fundamental changes in the industry were effected by the liberalisation which began to accompany it. It was agreed that there had to be some competition introduced, the beginnings of a challenge to the massive monopoly enjoyed by the nationalised telephone system. Privatised Cable & Wireless had telephone interests overseas. They now stepped forward, happy to set up a rival operation called Mercury, offering in the first instance a much more competitive service to big business especially in the City of London. From these humble beginnings the British telecommunications market was gradually opened up to a host of new companies and technologies.

The transformation was breathtaking. Before privatisation it was not possible to buy a telephone: British domestic customers could only rent phones and there was a very limited choice of style and colour of handset. The monopolist tried to defend the monopoly at every twist and turn. Liberalisers were told that if private companies and individuals were allowed to buy their own equipment and add it to the system it would 'damage the network'. It was a typically absurd proposition. BT was saying that people would make businesses out of selling equipment to others. There were legal protections against people adding such equipment as well. The monopolists tried to argue that the introduction of competition would serve to increase costs and prices. They argued that the introduction of even a single competitor in the form of Mercury would cream off the most lucrative business, the inter-city business from the City of London and the other large business centres for example, and leave BT with nothing that could be profitable.

The government did not accept any of these self-serving arguments. Indeed, within a matter of a few years, the management of privatised BT themselves became strong advocates of competition, wishing to become challengers and competitors elsewhere in the world and accepting that competition could be good for their business even at home. In the 1970's, investment in the telephone network in Britain was a matter for debate with the Treasury and government ministers. There were often occasions when the telephone system suffered as a result. Managers of it would have liked to have spent more, modernised their switchgear and extended their capacity more rapidly than public expenditure constraints allowed. Once BT and its rivals were in the private sector there was a step change in the amount of investment made. Since privatisation and liberalisation there has been massive investment in several competing mobile telephone networks. There has been an almost complete transition from mechanical and electrical switching to electronic. There has been a big build up in the amount of fibre optic cable installed and a huge expansion in the general capacity of the British network to take voice and data. Had British Telecom remained in the public sector with a monopoly, it is undeniably the case that there would have been much less investment, much less choice and the danger that BT might have backed one or two new technologies that were not as successful as the ones which the market has brought through to great popularity.

It is difficult to deny that the provision of telephone services is a public service. It is also difficult now to find anyone who believes that such a public service should be returned to state ownership or should be returned to monopoly from competition. The Labour Party in Britain was in favour of its re-nationalisation in the early days, but soon dropped it realising both that it would be far too expensive to deal with compensation and would be an unpopular move given the big improvements and price reductions achieved under private ownership. Today phones can be installed within twenty-four or forty-eight hours of the request: there are no more six-month waits. Today people can choose from a stunning array of equipment and can buy their own rather than having to hire or lease. Today people can switch from one telecoms operator to another overnight if they see a better service and a cheaper price.

The transport industries

The transport industries in Britain have not seen such a decisive battle between the advocates of competitive free enterprise and the advocates of state monopoly intervention and control. We have a curious mixed economy in Britain that is causing many of the features that we experienced in the telephone networks of the late 1970's. Just as with telephones in the 1970's, so with roads and railways today there is an acute shortage of capacity. There is a shortage of money for expanding capacity owing to the tight controls placed by the government on the private sector and more especially by the restrictions on public finance for the crucial parts of the transport network that are publicly owned. Just as in telecommunications in the 1970's there was a lack of imagination, an unwillingness to catch up with the new technologies and choices available in more advanced countries like the USA, so in the case of transport provision in areas controlled or regulated by the government, there is that same lack of panache and interest in the customer today.

Of all the passenger miles travelled by British people, 87% are travelled in private vehicles. The public has been voting with its feet over many years, showing that it wishes to carry out as much of its travel as possible in a privatised, flexible system of transport. The main problem individuals encounter when trying to use the flexibility of their car to maximum effect is the poor standard and low capacity of the road system which is provided as a public sector monopoly offered free at the point of use. Transport has become the chosen battleground within the Labour party over whether to move more in the direction of free enterprise, or move back towards more public monopoly. It is here, in transport, that we see the most experimentation with Third Way finance, trying to find a system that is neither wholly private nor wholly public. It is here that we see most movement both ways, as the government shows it lacks a coherent approach to how travel should be financed and regulated.

The arguments against road transport

The government puts forward two important public interest arguments which seem to drive practically its whole policy towards motoring and the provision of road capacity. The first is the argument that road transport is a major polluter and that something should be done to limit road transport in order to try to cut pollution. The second is that too many people die or are injured on the roads and that this is nearly always the fault of the drivers of private sector vehicles. This too leaves the government to conclude that there should be less private transport, that private transport should take place at slower speeds and under many more restrictions.

The government needs to examine why it is there has been such a persistent surge in car ownership and use, despite many efforts to prevent this occurring. The figures of growth are themselves remarkable. In 1950 there were just two million cars registered in the United Kingdom, with only one in seven of all households being able to afford one. By 1998 the number of cars registered was over 21.5 million vehicles. Seven out of ten households owned at least one car. In the richer parts of the country we are now witnessing the three or four car family with every teenager clamouring to own or use a vehicle as soon as they have passed their driving test and with both husband and wife feeling they need cars to give them flexibility to do their own jobs and to play their own part in family life.

Since 1950 car traffic has grown fifteen-fold whilst bus traffic has remained relatively static and train travel has been in strong relative decline until privatisation. People are telling the government by their actions and, by their willingness to pay ever- higher taxes on motoring, that they value the flexibility the motorcar brings enormously.

Emissions from motor vehicles

It is quite true that emissions from road traffic were becoming unacceptable during the early 1990's during a period of very rapid growth in road vehicle usage. Since 1990 the impact of better technology and stronger regulation has begun to be felt. The British government, along with partners in Europe, have brought in successive regulations that offer tighter and tighter controls upon the amount of unpleasant material that cars and commercial vehicles are allowed to emit. On 31 December 1992 they introduced the first standard for passenger cars followed in October 1993 by a standard for heavy diesel engines and in October 1994 for light commercial vehicles. These standards were tightened between 1996 and 1997 in a second round of regulation, tightened again in a third round on 1 January 2001 and are scheduled to be tightened further in a fourth round coming in on 1 January 2006. The changes are dramatic, slashing the emission of carbon monoxide, hydrocarbons and nitrogen oxides by more than 90%. (See Table One in Appendix One)

The introduction of regulation takes time. Manufacturers of vehicles need to be given an adjustment period to meet the new standards. It can then take many years before all the cars or commercial vehicles in the car park are changed for modern ones meeting the higher standards. The main residual problem we have with the emission of carbon monoxide, hydrocarbons, oxides of nitrogen and particulates, the things that most worry people and are most likely to cause lung and bronchial disorders, now come from older vehicles. In 1997 it was estimated that over 80% of all the oxides of nitrogen and particulate emissions from cars came from cars manufactured before 1993. The contribution of buses is also a matter of grave concern as the majority of the bus fleet is still made up of vehicles constructed before even the first round of new standards came in.

There has been a long running battle between the advocates of diesel and petrol engines. Although the unpleasant emissions from both petrol and diesel have been progressively reduced and are reducing, thanks to regulation and technical improvements, diesel engines are responsible for more of the unpleasant substances than petrol engines when comparing like with like. On the other hand petrol vehicles produce more carbon dioxide than diesel engines. Given the understandable health worries about the emissions of particulates and oxides of nitrogen there is a lot to be said for the petrol engine, especially in urban areas where the heavy concentration of diesel fumes can be particularly unpleasant and dangerous.

There are many possibilities for the future to make even more progress in cutting down every type of emission from flexible motor transport. The high price of fuel is leading motor manufacturers and some customers to find new ways of encouraging much greater fuel efficiency. A pioneering Honda vehicle which combines electric technology with a traditional petrol engine can lift miles per gallon to an average of around 80. The industry is beginning to explore the idea of automatic cut-out of engines when cars are stationary at junctions or in heavy traffic and looking at mixed methods of powering cars along the Honda lines. In due course there may be even more breakthroughs with electric vehicles producing a better power to weight ratio capable of meeting more commercial and passenger needs. Motor manufacturers are working on water as a fuel, driving the car by generating hydrogen. Great progress is already being made with different types of fuel. Lead petrol has now been banned, meaning there is now no lead pollution problem whatsoever as a result of motor traffic. Ultra-low sulphur petrol and diesel is being progressively introduced cutting vehicle emissions still further.

One of the paradoxes of the government's position is that the single most important way in which emissions could be cut would be by allowing people to make more uninterrupted journeys at steady speed. Fuel consumption and therefore unpleasant emissions greatly increase when a vehicle has to stop and start and proceed in low gear at slow speeds for long periods. Urban pollution is greatly increased by many of the so called traffic management measures introduced which serve to slow down or impede the flow of vehicles in principal roads in towns and cities. The government, as so often, is speaking with forked tongue, urging us to be much more aware of the impact of burning fuel upon the environment whilst at the same time taking other measures which guarantee we will have to burn more of it whether we travel by car or bus in congested urban areas.

Sometimes in the government's propaganda they seem to forget that all forms of transport produce emissions and that public transport produces relatively high levels of emission due to the age of the vehicles. Anyone watching a diesel multiple-unit train waiting at a station with all its engines running will know just how much visible particulate pollution comes out of such a train. Unless the train is absolutely packed with passengers it generates much more pollution per passenger travelling than if the passengers on the train were all taken in modern fuel-efficient cars on the same journey. Similarly, buses remain much bigger polluters vehicle for vehicle than passenger cars. Even if an older bus were completely full it would still be beneficial to the environment to take everyone off the bus and take him or her in cars designed to modern emission standards, as this would cut the per capita pollution of their travel.

Critics of the car have to accept that we have made far more dramatic strides in cutting the unpleasant pollution from cars than from any other kind of human activity which burns hydrocarbons. Ever willing, however, to knock the car they counter by saying that nonetheless petrol cars remain a very important source of CO_2 emissions and that these are going to devastate the planet through global warming. The government, in its study of the environmental impact of vehicle use, very helpfully put all this into context. Its figures show that in 1996 industry accounted for 30% of CO_2 emissions, domestic residences for 25%, road transport for 22% and commercial institutions for 14%. Far from being the predominant or most problematic emitter of CO_2 these figures demonstrate that road transport is only the third worst but is the one that is subject to most regulatory control. It is true that the energy supply industry offers the most scope to cut CO_2 emissions significantly. Any further switch to gas fired electricity generation from coal would make a significant contribution whilst if the government did wish to switch more energy production to nuclear and non-fossil fuel the impact would be even more dramatic.

Out of the 22% of CO_2 emissions that come from road transport a little over half come from petrol cars whilst buses account for 4%, heavy goods vehicles for 23%, light goods vehicles for 10.5% and diesel cars for a further 7%. This means that private cars as a whole account for some 13% of CO_2 emissions. It is of course important to make progress in reducing this. The EU has produced new controls to make substantial reductions in the amount of CO_2 emission permitted by each new car sold over the next few years. As the figures reveal, however, to make a really big impact on CO_2 emissions it is necessary to tackle a series of other problems over and above the motorcar. Indeed, given the poor efficiency of many domestic central heating systems it is probably the case that if people turned off the heating in their home and got into a small, modern, fuel-efficient car and drove around with the heating on that they would be cutting the amount of pollution they were contributing to the environment. They would certainly be cutting that pollution if they turned all the lights off at the same time when they left home. A substantial part of the CO_2 emission into the atmosphere is the combined impact of electricity generation and domestic heating systems. In both these areas there need to be substantial strides in improving the efficiency of boilers, in changing the method of generation and greatly increasing thermal insulation to cut down the need for fuel burn at all.

One of the oddest things about the present government policy towards the environment is how lopsided it is. As an enthusiastic environmentalist who would like to help clean up the planet, I am as keen as the next person that new generations of vehicles should only produce a fraction of the harmful emissions that previous vehicles did. We are well within sight of meeting this target that can be achieved by a mixture of regulatory pressure and tax incentive. I would like to see similar energy and enthusiasm on curbing the dangerous emissions of the domestic boiler, and encouraging far more thermal insulation in all public and private buildings to make a substantial reduction in the amount of energy we burn. This would make a far bigger impact on harmful emissions than attempting to tax or price some cars off the road.

Technology, not taxation, is the way to clean up the transport sector. Regulatory stick is being used to considerable effect to produce new generations of private cars which are so much cleaner than their predecessors. A modern car is between thirty and fifty times cleaner than the equivalent vehicle of a decade ago, an astonishing improvement but much needed. Tax incentives have been extremely effective in encouraging people to take up greener fuels at the petrol pump. The next stage is to have a policy to encourage people to renew their vehicles, thereby getting rid of the older vehicles in the British car park more rapidly. The most important difference we could make to air pollution generated by road transport would be to renew all vehicles more than seven years old as soon as possible or, in the case of valuable classics, to modify them to bring them up to modern standards where people wish to use them in the normal course of business.

It would be a good idea to offer people a tax incentive to scrap old vehicles. Why shouldn't the government announce that anyone prepared to scrap an old vehicle completely would be allowed to buy an equivalent vehicle free of tax on the purchase price? This could make a major impact on the problem, bringing new vehicles into the affordable category for far more people and accelerating the scrappage rate of old polluting vehicles dramatically.

It should also be a priority of government policy to see a similar renewal of the bus and train fleet, now proportionately far dirtier than the private car. We will examine in due course how investment in the railways and bus industry can be accelerated through private capital which in turn could make an important contribution to cutting airborne pollution.

Safety

The second big argument used against the motorcar is the argument of safety. The government are quite right in saying that 702 people killed on the roads in 1999 and 4,714 seriously injured on trunk roads is unacceptable. The good news is that fatalities and serious injuries have been declining over the last decade despite a surge in traffic growth. Figures also show that motorways and trunk roads are far safer than smaller local roads.

This evidence seems to be in contradiction to the government's belief that the prime problem with road safety is speed. Of course it is true that if vehicles went at no speed at all there would be no accidents because they would all be stationary. What the government has in mind is to try to lower running speeds from 70mph to 50mph or from 50mph to 40mph or from 40mph to 30mph or from 30mph to 20mph. The sad fact is that if a car or lorry hits another or hits a pedestrian when travelling at these speeds, even the low ones, there will be at least an injury and in all too many cases there will be serious injuries or fatalities. If a child steps off a pavement close to an approaching vehicle travelling at twenty or thirty miles an hour it is likely that child will still be killed or seriously injured as the driver will have no opportunity, given response time and braking distance, to stop. Similarly, if a heavy lorry hits a small car side on even if the lorry is only doing twenty miles an hour the weight of the impact is quite likely to do serious damage to the passenger or driver.

If looked at more sensibly, speed is not usually the cause of motor accidents. Drivers can travel at their fastest on motorways, yet motorways are by far and away the safest roads. The reason motorways are much safer is to do with their design and junctions. On motorways we do not permit any pedestrians, cyclists or low-powered motorised bicycles. We segregate traffic flowing in one direction from traffic flowing in the other, and we have no crossroads or roundabouts. By removing difficult junctions, segregating traffic, and preventing conflict between motor vehicles and other types of road user we achieve far safer routes.

Bad driving is the most obvious general cause of accidents. Bad driving could include driving at a speed inappropriate to the conditions. If someone decides to break a 30mph speed limit and travel at 70mph on a congested urban road they are very likely to come to grief and to do damage to other road users. This is fortunately a very uncommon experience. A far more common cause of accidents is careless driving at road junctions. Sometimes people pull out at road junctions because they are thinking of something else, or sometimes they take a badly calculated risk. More accidents to pedestrians are caused by careless reversing, often because the driver has a restricted view but proceeds nonetheless, than are caused by pure speed. It is important that government and local government should do all in their power to try and cut the volume of accidents and the misery that causes for many families. Instead of concentrating on speed it would be far better to concentrate on a number of simpler measures that could make a more direct impact upon the number of collisions.

Pedestrians need pavements, cars need roads

Firstly, wherever possible we should avoid contact between pedestrians and cars. In the USA pedestrians are not permitted to jaywalk on the carriageway of the road or to cross the road other than at organised crossing points. In most towns and cities in Britain now there are a large number of properly organised crossing points. It is best to cross a road at a traffic light controlled junction as in the United States. At such a light controlled junction it is safe to cross when the traffic on the road you are crossing is stationary, obeying a red light. Safety can be enhanced by separate pedestrian light indicators to show when it is best to cross. There are also a number of other pedestrian crossings. The designs of some of these are far from perfect with pedestrians and drivers sometimes playing a dangerous game of chicken with each other as to whether the pedestrian has yet started on the crossing or not. Consideration should be given to redesign so that it is clearer when the driver has a duty to stop and clearer when the pedestrian has a duty to wait.

Cycling

Secondly, as a cyclist myself I know how dangerous it can be for cyclists on relatively narrow and highly congested carriageways. To the driver, a cyclist who wobbles round a drain cover or a pothole is a constant fear. For the cyclist, a driver who overtakes too close is a constant worry. Wherever possible we should provide a segregated cycleway, preferably divided from the main carriageway by a physical barrier. This cannot be done in congested areas where the roads are already narrow but it can be done where there is more pavement space than we need for typical pedestrian usage or where the carriageway of the road is more than adequate for wide vehicles.

Better junctions

A third priority should be redesign of junctions. Wherever possible, where space permits, traffic going right, left and straight on should be segregated into different lanes. This reduces the average amount of time traffic has to queue to proceed across a busy junction and thereby reduces driver tension which, in its turn, will reduce the propensity of drivers to take unreasonable risks. At light-controlled junctions it should be possible to allow drivers to turn left on a red, treating the red light as a stop sign and only proceeding when the road is clear. In some cases stop sign junctions would be safer as light-controlled junctions. In all cases light-controlled junctions would be more effective if they were sensitive to relative traffic flows from the different directions approaching the junction to minimise delay for travellers. The more drivers are delayed the more likely they are to become frustrated and the more likely they are to take unreasonable risks at junctions as a result.

Designing out unsafe roads

Fourthly, road design should be examined everywhere with a view to designing out the most obvious danger spots and faults. For example, on blind bends road widening should be carried out to reduce the blindness of the bend. Where this is physically impossible, proper mirrors should be fitted so that drivers can see around the corner at all stages in both directions. Where roads have been artificially narrowed to force two lanes into one increasing the likelihood of head-on collisions this should be designed out of the structure.

Improving car safety

Fifthly, motor manufacturers should be encouraged to make further design improvements to encourage safety. Substantial strides have been made since the 1950's and 1960's to improve the safety of passenger cars. Particular attention has been paid to improving the safety of driver and passengers in each vehicle. The introduction of seatbelts on each seat coupled with legislation requiring their wear has greatly reduced the numbers of drivers and passengers injured following sudden braking or collision. The introduction of airbags and padded interiors has also helped to reduce damage to driver and passengers when the vehicle stops too suddenly or is damaged from outside in a collision. Some progress has been made in reducing the number of sharp edges and hard protuberances on the exterior of cars to give other vehicles and pedestrians more of a chance in the event of a collision. More vehicles could be designed with softer sections at the front and the rear that collapse progressively in a collision whilst keeping a rigid middle section to give the passengers reasonable protection. The more energy that can be absorbed by the front and rear thirds of the vehicle, the better for the sake of the other vehicle or people involved.

Trunk road junctions

Sixth, on trunk roads we need to give priority to further junction improvements. Wherever possible we need grade-separated interchanges which transform the accident rates by removing opportunity for conflict at junctions between traffic moving in different directions.

Pedestrian routes

Seventh, we need to make sure that there are good, straightforward, easy pedestrian routes wherever possible and especially for people to carry out regular journeys. Sometimes new pavements, walkways, pedestrian bridges, underpasses and other facilities should be provided. Pedestrians get very impatient in Britain if they have to wait at all before crossing a road. In busy areas there should be an option. Those who wish to cross the road should have reasonable access to a light-controlled junction enabling them to pass on green, perhaps entailing a wait. They should also be offered the choice of a bridge or underpass so that they can cross the road directly without having to experience any delay. Pedestrians should be able to live in secure knowledge that cars and vans do not drive on pavements and this rule should be strictly enforced. Motorists should be able to live with reasonable confidence that pedestrians do not walk on busy highways unless they are at a proper junction with a pedestrian-controlled route.

Protection of school children

Eighth, we do need severe restrictions on cars adjacent to schools at the morning and afternoon arrival and departure of children, especially at primary schools. Whilst of course young children should be supervised by adults and older children should be properly trained in kerb drill, all parents and grandparents would want to see proper steps taken to minimise the risk to children and grandchildren outside schools. This should entail clear warnings and much lower speeds at the time of the morning and evening arrival and exodus from school. There is no need to keep these restrictions on cars in place at other times of the day and especially no need during school holidays and at weekends.

Safer reversing

Ninth, motor manufacturers could be required to take the problem of unsafe reversing more seriously. Better design of motor vehicles to give more visibility to the rear would help. We need to consider better mirrors and see whether it is possible to produce a cheap version of the rear camera technology. This enables the driver to have a clear and unimpeded view of the rear through a lens placed at a suitable vantage point on the tail of the vehicle. We could also consider more general fitting of proximity warning systems to motor vehicles to minimise the risk of hitting street furniture, buildings, other vehicles or people.

Much of safety is common sense. It will never be possible to legislate to prevent all accidents. If only it were. We are all human and any one of us may make a mistake as a driver, pedestrian or cyclist at any point. You cannot stop people driving or walking when pre-occupied or even when tired. It is a matter of judgment. You can stop people drinking or taking drugs and it is wise to make sure that these substances are not present in sufficient quantities to represent a serious hazard.

The nine suggestions above are just a sample of the kind of things that could be done to try and design accidents out of roads, to improve the safety of vehicles and to reduce the potential for conflict between different road and pavement users. Pedestrians should be able to walk around towns and cities freely and unimpeded by road traffic wherever possible. Similarly drivers should have rights to use the principal roads in urban areas as well as outside at reasonable speed without fear of conflict with pedestrians. Many accidents now are caused by growing frustrations on both sides where both pedestrians and motorists take unreasonable risks because they do not wish to be delayed.

Tragic accidents also occur on the railways, on the seas and waterways and in the air. Some people are killed or maimed by public transport operators just as people are killed or maimed by private transport. The government has taken a very strong line on railway safety but in a way which has probably impeded the development and growth of the railways which tend to be a relatively safe form of surface transport. The railways should, of course, be much safer than roads because a strict segregation is in force. No member of the public is allowed to walk upon or near a railway line. No one is allowed to cross a railway line on foot unless at a scheduled level crossing when the gates allow it. Trains travelling in one direction are, in most cases, put on separate track from those travelling in another to avoid head on collision. The track itself constrains the train from wandering into the path of another. Above all, trains are strictly segregated by a series of signal controls. There is usually more than a mile separating one train from another on the same stretch of track, leading to fairly inefficient use of the railway line but understandable, given the complexities and difficulties of bringing a very heavy train to a halt should the need arise.

Despite these draconian measures to create a very safe railway, several problems remain. The first is that all too many train drivers ignore red light signals and take their train beyond the red light, sometimes directly into danger. Secondly, there have been two recent examples of motor vehicles crashing down embankments and landing up on the track without sufficient time to give warning or to clear the vehicle away. This has led directly to head-on collision owing to the poor braking times and long braking distances of trains. Thirdly, the enormous pressure and wear exerted on steel track particularly on gradients and at bends by fast moving heavy trains can lead to track fissures and cracks. This in turn can lead to a train being de-railed if its weight and speed is the immediate cause, or if the track has already snapped completely. Fourth, there are no seat belts fitted in UK trains. Where a train brakes suddenly or derails, passengers are flung violently around the carriages and sometimes out of the windows when the train breaks.

Obeying red signals on the railways

The first cause of accidents on the railways is the easiest to deal with. Better driver training and discipline should take care of much of the problem. Every road driver knows that shooting red lights is a dangerous thing to do and is clearly against the law. At many light controlled junctions on roads there are now cameras designed to deter or to ensure prosecution of the driver should he be foolish enough to ignore the warnings. We all accept that we have no right to shoot the red light if it is red in our direction, even if it is clearly safe to do so. We fully accept that we should be prosecuted and we have to patiently wait our time. The same should follow on the railways. Every train driver should know that shooting a red light is a serious offence and that action will follow as a result. A train driver cannot steer his train and does not have to think about route or direction. That is determined for him by the lay of the tracks and by the movement of the points. He is solely responsible for speeding up and slowing down and his main duty is to ensure that he always stops his train at every red light and at every station where he is scheduled to stop. Failure to perform this should be a serious matter. We should also bear in mind that the train driver is a paid professional whereas the car driver is usually an unpaid amateur.

The government has decided that more elaborate electronic systems in train cabs could do the job for the driver. This could indeed represent a further way of solving the problem, although it is important to make sure that firstly the technology really does work and the train will always stop at the red light for the driver will come to rely on it and secondly, the technology works well enough so that the train is not stopped without cause.

Car barriers near railway lines

The second problem may require remedial works at various bridges and viaducts to make it more difficult for a badly driven vehicle to career down an embankment onto the track. Drivers do know that it is an extremely serious offence to end up on a railway line and have seen what happens if they do so and stay alive. The recent, successful prosecution led to a prison sentence for the offender. This, however, will not prevent such an event happening again in the future if there is a physical route for a car or lorry to get on to a train track by careering down an embankment. The problem in such circumstances is the vehicle may well be damaged in such a way that it cannot be moved again under its own power, having reached the bottom and the track bed. There may be no way off the track bed for the vehicle even if it is still functioning. It is best, therefore, to spend some more money on providing stronger physical barriers at such weak points where the rail system overlaps with the road system.

Different rail technology

The third problem is the most difficult to solve as it is inherent in the nature of rail technology itself, that there is always the risk of steel rail cracking and always the risk of derailment for one reason or another. Further consideration will be given to the technological advantages of current train systems at a later stage. It is important that we use the best possible tracing technology to investigate steel rail on a continuous and regular basis in order to try and avoid the sort of disasters we saw at Hatfield. Fit seat belts in trains. This would save lives and injuries when trains do crash.

Neither safety nor pollution provides knockout arguments against using a flexible form of personal travel. People have shown, by their purchasing patterns and by their travel arrangements, that they desperately want a personalised system of travel that gets them from their home to their desired destination as easily as possible. The car has so many advantages over other forms of public transport that it is not at all surprising that most people rely heavily upon it and many young people whilst being enthusiastic environmentalists are desperate to take their driving test and to join the great car society.

My car is never late for me but I can be as late as I like for my car. It sits patiently in my garage at home awaiting my pleasure. When I get to my journey's end it will be there, awaiting my return. I am not allowed to be late for public transport but all too often public transport is late for me. Public transport does not come to my door and is often not available close at hand. Very often I need to make several connections to complete a journey on public transport. Usually my car is capable of taking me from where I start to my destination without needing any further mode of transport, other than a short walk, to complete the task.

A car doubles up as a shopping trolley, a delivery van, a mobile office and a waiting room. If I am waiting for a bus or sometimes a train I can get very cold and in many cases very wet. My car protects me from the elements at all times. If I wish to go to London and stay there for a couple of days I can put in my books, papers, food, clothing and any other equipment that I may need for my expedition. The boot and floor space in the back of the car will swallow it all up quite comfortably. If I wish to carry out a similar journey by bus or train there would be strict limits on what I could manage to carry to the bus stop or train station and strict limits on how much the train or bus would be prepared to take in the limited space available on public transport for luggage.

If you live in the centre of a big city like London it is possible to live without a car and not feel restricted or hemmed in. People who do so often say they cannot understand why the rest of us need cars. Any examination of their travel habits shows, however, that they are as dependent on the motor vehicle as the rest of us, albeit in different ways. Many Londoners regularly use taxis to get about in London itself. If they wish to make a foray out into the countryside they often hire cars for the weekend. Most of the goods that they buy in the shops or are delivered to their homes are delivered by van or lorry. It is a very rare person who lives in a city without a car and goes everywhere on foot or by bike, or by train and bus. There is no-one, even the most avid enthusiast for public transport in the city, who can lead their current life without the motor vehicle, as so much of the supply system is currently based on the internal combustion engine of the van and the lorry. It is our task now to examine how the capacity of all our different transport networks can be expanded without doing grave damage to the beautiful places that remain in our green island.

Chapter five

BRITAIN'S RAILWAYS –
THIRD CLASS NOT THIRD WAY

History

BRITAIN IS FAMOUS FOR her railways. The country was a railway pioneer from the early nineteenth century onwards. All the main railway lines were built by private companies raising private capital in the market place. Steel wagons running on steel rails began in the coal industry as a means of moving coal from the pithead. The introduction of steam locomotives created the conditions to begin the railway boom. The first public railway using steam locomotives linked Stockton and Darlington.

Railway mania

Between 1829 and 1830 the railway world was transformed. In October 1829, the Liverpool and Manchester railway held the Rainhill Trials and eleven months later opened the new line. It rapidly became a commercial success and fuelled the first wave of railway enthusiasm. In the three years from 1833 to 1835 some 550 miles of new track were authorised. New railway companies usually announced their intention to issue shares of a nominal value of £100 each, requiring only a small deposit of £5. The remainder of the money was called as needed during construction. Issuing geared shares like this encouraged more speculative interest. Between 1836 and 1837, 1,500 new miles of track were authorised before the first big promotional boom came to an end. There were difficulties sometimes in collecting the money and a number of devices like paying interest on dividends and issuing attractive and sometimes geared preference shares and loan notes were introduced to oil the wheels of finance. Regulation caught up with paying interest on dividends, which was outlawed in 1847, and the issue of preference shares and issuing loan notes was prohibited in 1844.

By the early 1840's some disappointment set in. Far from achieving dividends in excess of 10%, as many had anticipated, only a handful of companies were paying more than 4%. Nonetheless, they usually paid more than the rate of return on government Stock after interest rates fell in 1842.

The second wave of enthusiasm broke out in the middle 1840's.

By the end of 1845 commentators listed 1,000 railway schemes with a total capital of over £700 million illustrating the size of the enthusiasm. It was about this time that amalgamation started amongst the pioneering companies to create territorial monopolies. In 1844, the Midland Railway was born out of the three companies centring on Derby. The London and North Western was formed from combining the Grand Junction itself with the Liverpool and Manchester, the London and Birmingham and the Manchester and Birmingham. In 1845 2,816 new railway miles were authorised and in 1846 a new peak was achieved of 4,541.

In the 1860's in another boom for railway promotion and construction, the railway contractors expanded their activities beyond civil engineering. In some cases the contractor would agree to build the line in return for taking payment in the company's securities. Another method of financing construction was through the issue of Lloyd's Bonds. The railway company incurred a debt by giving the creditor one of the bonds, which guaranteed payment at a future date. In the three decades from the early 1840's, over 13,000 new railway miles were added to the network and money invested increased from £60 million to £530 million.

The bulk of the railway network was completed by the 1870's with 15,000 route miles up and running. Between then and 1914, a further 8,000 miles were added, making a complete network of 23,000 miles. In this later period, much of the Underground system was built in London and the Manchester, Sheffield & Lincolnshire railway was linked to the capital. Route capacity was raised in many parts of the network especially by quadrupling tracks.

Government control and decline
The First World War changed the industry fundamentally. In 1914 the Railway was taken over by the government under the powers of the Regulation of the Forces Act 1871. The Railway Executive Committee, first formed in 1912 from the general managers of the major companies, was given the task of managing and operating the industry during the period of state control. The companies remained in private hands but the government directed the overall service. The government paid the companies amounts of money based on their monthly estimates of the costs, which included an allowance for maintenance work. The government met all wage increases and paid a 4% return on capital expenditure undertaken since 1913. This wartime control system lasted until 1921.

Some thought that the exercise in central control was excellent. However, this was not the passengers' experience. Passenger services were withdrawn or severely cut back whilst even goods traffic for the private sector had to stand in the queue, making sure that all government and troop requirements were met first. In 1921 the Railways Act produced a very different private sector railway. Four mainline companies survived the reorganisation and the Railway Rates Tribunal was set up to supervise charging. 120 separate railway companies were compulsorily merged into four, each with a territorial monopoly. The creation of the monopoly required stronger regulation to try and limit its abuses. Railway charges were fixed at levels to provide a profit related to what they were enjoying in 1913. This new arrangement of central direction was meant to avoid the so-called 'costs of competition' and bring the advantages of planning. It was not what the passengers thought. Partly because of the way the railways were organised and partly because of the growing challenge of motor transport, passenger journeys started a dramatic fall between the two great wars. In 1921 there were 1,787 million passenger journeys. This fell to 1,651 million in 1927 and to 1,295 million in 1938. The Second World War saw similar arrangements to those of the First World War, with the government taking control. The 1947 Transport Act, put through by the post war Labour government, nationalised all inland transport except private cars and certain lorries. All of the nationalised transport activities were put under the British Transport Commission. In 1953 the new Conservative government, through its Transport Act, denationalised road haulage, abolished the Railway Executive and initiated a reorganisation of the railways. Passenger miles continued their downward decline and large losses were chalked up.

Privatisation and growth

The Railways Act of 1993 took powers to restructure and privatise British Rail. Between 1995 and 1996 Railtrack was sold and the franchise offered to a series of new operating companies capable of running train services over the track. The government decided that it was right to shift all of the assets out of the public sector into the hands of new private owners. They also introduced some competition in the provision of train services by allowing competing companies to tender for franchises for a fixed period and allowing some choice between competing companies where lines and routes permitted. The government decided to leave the rail network itself in monopoly hands, transferring the assets to the new Railtrack plc in 1994, prior to sale.

Railway privatisation was always a contentious issue. The

traditional Labour position, strongly behind a nationalised monopoly, granting as they saw it, stronger bargaining powers to the trade unions involved, was hostile to any type of privatisation. Amongst those in favour of privatising the railways there was considerable debate about how it could best be done. Some favoured a return to the regional companies that had run the railways in the private sector before 1947; others favoured keeping the track in public ownership whilst transferring train running to private competing companies. Others favoured a mixture of regional companies and those specialising in different types of business such as freight.

The privatised industry took over a set of assets in pretty poor condition, a disenchanted travelling public and a long-term secular decline in train travel which had set in from 1914 onwards. There had been precious little good news for the railways throughout the twentieth century. The nineteenth century had been the great age of the steam train with any forward thinking person keen to see a railway line and station near his property bringing trade, people and prosperity. As the twentieth century advanced more and more people turned to the attractions of the more flexible motor vehicle and thought of locating their businesses closer to main arterial roads than railway lines. The more government strengthened its control over the industry as the twentieth century advanced the more the problem of declining use and a low quality of service became endemic. By the time of the privatisation debates in the middle 1990's most people seemed to have forgotten, or had never realised, that the heyday of the railway was a story of exuberant capitalism. Hundreds of projectors and companies had vied to establish themselves as the builders and owners of new sections of track, raising millions from the Stock Market to do so. The railway, which had seen a surge of new investment, new technology and growth in passenger and goods usage throughout the nineteenth century when it was a competitive, privately financed industry, saw a declining investment, an unsatisfactory service and a big decline in patronage in the twentieth century under government monopoly.

Critics were quite sure that things would get worse under privatisation. Yet from the mid 1990's, when the railway was broken up and shares were sold, things started to improve quite dramatically. In the first five years after privatisation passenger rail demand increased by 30%, an average growth rate of 6.3% per year. It was particularly strong for London's commuting travel. Similarly, there was a sharp surge in freight volumes, with the first five years showing a 40% increase, returning the market share of rail freight to mid 1980's levels following the decline.

The 1997 Labour government- regulation, then bankruptcy

The new government, elected in 1997, approached this success with a certain ambiguity. They wished to sustain an anti-privatisation rhetoric. In opposition they had opposed privatisation and, under the influence of their union friends and their own instincts, were keen to tell the public that anything that went wrong on the railways from now was the result of privatisation. On the other hand, they were wedded to the idea that more people and goods should travel by rail and less by road. They could not contain themselves in claiming credit for the surge in passenger usage and in goods freight that was being experienced month by month on the recently privatised railway. Throughout the first Parliament of the Labour government they said that the railways were now on the mend and were potentially very successful and told us that they had no intention of re-nationalising them. At the same time, they were very willing to continue to criticise the former privatisation, the previous Conservative government, and to attribute to privatisation any train crash or other operating problem that emerged. John Prescott, as Transport Secretary, was particularly worried about safety. He was not persuaded by the fact that the privatised railway industry killed and maimed slightly fewer people than the nationalised one had done. In a sense, it was wholly admirable that he sought ever-higher safety standards on the trains as none of us can countenance death by travel as a regular feature of our society. However, his great preoccupation with railway safety turned out to burden the industry with more difficulties than the road transport sector. This made sustaining the very good recovery of the early years after privatisation that much more difficult.

In the first couple of years of the new government they decided to cut capital expenditure financed by the state. In particular they reduced the expenditure on the tube and on new highways and began to study what could be done to bring about their dream of an integrated transport policy with public transport playing a bigger and bigger role. In July 2000, they brought out their first ten-year plan for British Transport called Transport 2010. The plan heralded £180 billion of expenditure over its period. Of this public expenditure would make up £132 billion. The public money comprised £64.7 billion of public investment capital and £58.6 billion of revenue subsidy. This was going to be augmented by a planned £56.3 billion of private investment. Private investment included investment in railways and the private finance element in public private partnerships for things like national and traffic services, but excluded all private investment in motor transport. To put the scale of the plan into context it is quite likely that British consumers will buy more than £180 billion of new passenger cars over the ten years of the plan. On top of that there will be huge private investment in lorries, garages, private roads and driveways, and a host of other projects to service the motor vehicle.

The railway part of the plan projected a 50% increase in passenger use and an 80% increase in rail freight. The plan promised improvements in service quality with more punctual and reliable trains and less overcrowding. It included the installation of new train safety systems, secure stations, increased capacity on the West Coast and East Coast Mainlines, a high speed Channel Tunnel rail link, improved commuter services into London and other cities, the upgrading of freight routes to major ports and better integration with other transport modes. To do this it promised £60.4 billion of total expenditure on railways of which £34 billion would come from the private sector, with the public money splitting roughly half and half between grants or investment and a subsidy of £11.3 billion. They decided to set up a Strategic Rail Authority to invest in the railway network and plan the overall approach. The Strategic Rail Authority was given the task of deciding what quality and capacity improvements were needed, seeking them from train operators when replacing existing passenger franchises and through contracts with Railtrack for new railway lines. The rail regulator was given the task of setting the level and structure of charges that Railtrack can make for access to the network and seeking to ensure the company did not abuse its monopoly position.

At the time of the plan the government was already struggling with the railways, discovering that there were still problems with massive cost overruns and delays in trying to bring about new projects. Railtrack had been working for some time on modernising the West Coast Main Line to speed up trains and provide more capacity. In December 1999, the company announced that the cost of the project had increased from the original estimate of £2,300 million to £5,800 million. The government decided that it needed to offer direct payments to Railtrack to help with the massive increase in costs on this project.

The Ladbroke Grove crash had its impact. A driver ignored a warning signal, causing the disaster. The government decided the right answer to this was not better driver training and discipline but an automatic system which would prevent trains from proceeding in this rash way. Such large expenditures that brought no direct additional revenues to the railway were not going to make it easier to sustain the railway on private finance alone.

The government's original £60 billion, ten-year plan included the completion of the Channel Tunnel rail link to St Pancras, the upgrade of the East Coast Mainline, the modernisation of the West Coast Mainline, the upgrade of the Great Western Mainline, the completion of Thameslink 2000 enhancing commuter services into London, the construction of the East London Line extensions, an increase in capacity on the London-Brighton, Chiltern and Trans Pennine Lines, an increase of freight capacity on routes to major ports like Felixstowe, Folkestone and Dover, the removal of strategic bottlenecks on the network, the installation of the train protection and warning system, the introduction of better rolling stock, removal of all slam door carriages and the building of a number of station improvements with greater coverage of CCTV. This was always an extremely ambitious programme. What struck me, reading it for the first time, was how little money the government was suggesting. £60 billion might sound a lot of money but it is only £6 billion a year for the whole railway network; that is not a lot when the government expects an increase of 50% in capacity. There was very little margin in it for some of the problems that were bound to occur, which unfortunately, occurred all too rapidly with the Hatfield and Potters Bar crashes and the decline in performance that followed.

In March 2001, the government reported its progress in the Department of the Environment, Transport and the Regions Annual Report. On 1 February 2001, the Strategic Rail Authority had become fully operational. The SRA had a big job of work to try and agree new franchises for many of the existing train operating companies. Their investment programmes were beginning to slow down, as they were uncertain about their future. The Department proudly reported that, before the Hatfield tragedy, rail passenger miles travelled had reached their highest level for over fifty years, reflecting the strong improvements of privatisation. The graphs they show in their annual report shows that the turnaround occurred almost immediately privatisation went through.

The government reported that overall rail safety was continuing to improve gradually year on year but this improvement had been overshadowed by accidents. They had to respond to the tragic death of thirty one people in the Ladbroke Grove train crash and to the four dead and thirty four injured in the Hatfield derailment when a section of steel rail fractured on a bend under the weight of the train.

The Hatfield accident caused by 'gauge corner cracking' sent a shockwave through the government and led to a massive programme of inspection accompanied by emergency speed restrictions across the network. Inspection revealed that sections of track were subject to hairline fractures. Steel rail is particularly prone to this on bends and gradients. The amount of the steel wheel of the train, which actually meets the track, reduces as the train goes round a bend. The additional heavy freight trains and fast express trains running on the privatised network were greatly increasing the number of trains imposing heavy stresses upon track. It was not always old track that shattered. New track was equally prone to this. What seemed to matter was the configuration of the track on its bed and the weight and speed of trains travelling over it. The stresses increase geometrically the faster the train goes and the heavier the train is. The more the government blamed Railtrack and the industry, the more Railtrack had to take a very defensive approach. Everyone knew there was the possibility that the government would introduce measures to prosecute directors of companies for corporate manslaughter if they did not take a very cautious line on safety matters. As a result, emergency action was taken after the Hatfield crash.

It is well described by the Chairman of the Rail Passengers' Committee for Southern England in her annual report for 2000-2001. She states: "after the Hatfield crash Railtrack imposed emergency speed restrictions while it inspected hundreds of miles of track for hairline cracks that might cause another train accident, and replaced defective rails. It had to be sure that the track was safe. Passengers accepted that safety must come first but the immediate result was sheer chaos. Journey times suddenly doubled or even trebled, trains stopped short of their destination and passengers found themselves waiting on cold platforms for another train – not knowing whether it would turn up at all, let alone when." Suddenly all the benign trends that had followed privatisation were brought to a halt. Rail punctuality and reliability plummeted. Passengers were put off and started diverting to other means of travel. The industry was faced with falling revenues. At the same time there were escalating demands on its cash to accelerate the programme of track renewal and the installation of safety mechanisms both by the network operator and by the train operating companies who felt some of the cold draught from the government's criticisms. By the end of

February 2001, 92% of services had been restored and passenger numbers started to rise again. Recovery was fastest in London and the south east where most rail travel is concentrated.

On 5 July 2001, Sir Alastair Morton reviewed the industry in his last Chairman's Statement from the Strategic Rail Authority. He was only allowed to preside over the body in its full executive role for a matter of months and his commentary is a wry analysis as he waited for his successor to take over and change much of what he had done. He described how it was not helpful to try and apportion blame for the Hatfield crash in the way that Ministers were doing. He urged that they concentrate on curing the cause. He explained that doubts were beginning "to circulate about the systems ability to recover" and drew attention to the delays in granting new franchises where he blamed the government. He repeated his former warnings of June 1999 and February 2000, that Railtrack did not have the financial and management resources to carry out the improvements needed. He was very critical of Railtrack. He said that they had resisted his idea of bringing in so-called 'special purpose vehicles' for external project management and off balance sheet financing of certain improvement programmes. Railtrack, in his view, then followed this up in April 2001 with a decision to give the leadership of virtually all improvement projects to others. By late May he pointed out that Railtrack were seeking additional money to meet its primary task. He queried whether the £34 billion of private money could now be raised given that Railtrack was in financial difficulties. This honest statement of the state of play did not go down well in government or Railtrack circles.

The bankruptcy of Railtrack

The government brought in a new chairman, Richard Bowker, and set to work on new proposals following their General Election victory in summer of 2001. Stephen Byers replaced John Prescott as Secretary of State for the renamed Department of Transport, Local Government and the Regions. Railtrack soon presented him with their visiting card and explained their financial dilemma. Railtrack's revenues were badly hit by the post Hatfield crisis. This had reduced the amount of income coming in from the train operating companies using their track and had increased the number of payments Railtrack had to make in the form of compensation to the train operating companies for all the delays and cancellations that had come about. At the same time Railtrack was having to increase its expenditure more rapidly to deal with the problems of gauge corner cracking which the Hatfield crash had revealed. It was discovering further cost overruns and escalations on its major capital projects like the West Coast Mainline.

Railtrack could fairly say that a lot of the extra expenditure and some of the loss of revenue was a direct result of the government's regulatory interference with the railway. The government could correctly say that the company was still paying dividends when it needed all the cash it could obtain. The company had to bear substantial responsibility for the Hatfield crash, as it had not succeeded in checking the state of its rails carefully enough.

In normal circumstances, after a lively set of exchanges, a deal would have been done. The government could easily have insisted upon cancellation or substantial reduction of the dividend. Railtrack would undoubtedly have agreed to this under pressure. The government could have insisted on a strengthening of the safety function at Railtrack and required changes at board level to claim that lessons had been learned. Again Railtrack was likely to accept this. For its part a normal government would have seen that Railtrack did need additional money and that some of this money would have to come from the public purse. It had to spend a great deal on safety items required by the Regulator that would do nothing to raise the revenue of the business. Instead, the Secretary of State decided that his best course of action was to use his power under the Railways Act to put Railtrack into receivership. Discussions and negotiations continued on and off across the summer. In the autumn the government decided that it had done enough preparatory work to take the necessary action. One weekend in October it went to court and petitioned that Railtrack be put into administration. The company, the shareholders and many independent commentators were stunned by the speed and finality of this decision.

The reactions showed how much ideological division there still is over the vexed question of whether private or public money and management should be used to run the railways. The Labour Left and many of the government's supporters and commentators were cock-a-hoop. They saw it as back door renationalisation. They ignored the fact that the government claimed throughout that the intention was to return the company to private sector owners after a period in administration and ignored the fact that Railtrack was still technically a private sector company controlled by private sector accountants handling the receivership. To them it meant that the railway would effectively be under government control and drew a line under the period of private ownership, which they despised.

For the government's critics it was an act of madness which was bound to lead to much higher levels of public spending and public subsidy and was likely to lead to a sharp deterioration in the short term performance of the railway. It would disrupt and delay investment programmes and create difficulties in attracting the private finance necessary to implement the ten-year plan.

Stephen Byers discovered in the House of Commons that he was suddenly popular with many Labour backbenchers. He told them that the government's intention was to create a company limited by guarantee. This would be a private sector company with shareholders but it would be a 'not for profit' company that would pay no dividends. The intention would be to finance the improvements necessary in the rail network by bonds issued by the new company. Many Labour MPs chose to interpret this as being a kind of nationalised industry.

Railtrack in administration

Meanwhile the situation in the railway industry and in the City deteriorated much as many critics had predicted. It became extremely difficult to get agreement to any new investment projects. The government had to announce that it was making £3,500 million available in the five-month period up to the end of the financial period ending in March 2002. The administrator could really name any sum he needed and the government had to comply. Passengers discovered that there were continuing delays and difficulties. A number of good engineers left Railtrack in disgust and shareholders decided to investigate taking legal action against the government for the confiscation of their assets. When Railtrack subsequently reported healthy profits there was considerable surprise. Railtrack had not been to the government to tell them they were loss making and going under. They had gone to the government saying there would be problems in financing the very large programme of capital renewals and new investment that they and the government had been planning. In government statements this had been transformed into an assumption that Railtrack was a badly run, loss making business about to go bust. As the government sought to explain its position City investors wrote in no uncertain terms that they were furious at the bankruptcy of Railtrack. From now on the availability of private finance would be much more limited, problematic and expensive than before this watershed event.

In January 2002, some eighteen months after the government first issued its ten-year overall transport plan, the SRA issued its strategic plan. Comparing the two documents showed how little progress had been made. The Chairman began by saying "this strategic plan is the start, but it is not the end....we have to rediscover the service ethos and an accountable delivery culture, rediscover industry wide investment planning and rediscover how to train, manage and motivate our people so that the team works together like an efficient machine". The Chairman was by implication damning much that had gone before and was doing little to immediately rebuild the shattered morale of the industry. His report then degenerated into farce. He wrote: "I want to see fewer accountants, fewer lawyers and fewer consultants. Instead I want to see more engineers, more operators, more project managers and especially more young graduates, apprentices and school leavers joining an industry with a future". Over the last couple of years there has been a profusion of consultancies, lawsuits, legal advice and accountancy reviews. He wrote this at a time when senior accountants were running the industry through the administration of Railtrack. The government had employed no fewer than twenty-two different consultants to advise on the railway industry in the preceding year and the government itself faced possible law suits from Railtrack's shareholders and from the Mayor and Transport for London over the planned arrangements for the tube.

He stated: "I shall also be turning my attention to the investment planning framework for Britain's railway, which I am convinced is not currently fit for purpose. We need one plan, where all costs, benefits and risks associated with investing in rail can be clearly identified and analysed. Creation of this investment-planning framework is a key target for 2002". In other words the new chairman of the government's own appointed agency stated, more than eighteen months after the first ten-year plan was issued, that there was no satisfactory plan of any kind for developing Britain's railway and no satisfactory way to raise private finance, something he regards as a priority.

The new SRA has decided that it wants only one operator going into each of the London termini. As twenty-five franchises were created in the early years of privatisation this will require a merger mania to reduce the number of franchises and companies. Far from accelerating private investment into the industry this is likely to cause considerable delay and uncertainty with many companies saying they will not commit major new investment until they know whether or not they are a survivor from the purge. He announced the need to restructure the SRA completely to change the way in which it is managed. This is particularly surprising as the SRA is the government's own creature and Sir Alastair Morton, its first chairman, was the government's own choice.

The SRA has understood that 70% of all passenger journeys made nationally use the network in the south east. To allow the growth they are forecasting to take place without unacceptable over-crowding they are seeking longer trains, longer platforms and increased track capacity in the London area.

The SRA and the government agreed, following reductions in freight access charges and other adverse regulatory decisions, to increase the amount of public money available for the railways from £29.1 billion in the original 'ten year plan' to £33.5 billion. Following the bankruptcy of Railtrack, both the government and the SRA moved with the rail regulator to increase their hold over the planning framework of the industry. Just as the government had done in the two World Wars so today the government and its chosen arms, the SRA and the rail regulator, decided they needed centralised planning. They want centralised evaluation of investment projects and overall control over the special purpose vehicles, which will be established to bring in private finance to design, build and develop improvement projects for the network.

Already the strain is showing as the further improvements to the West Coast Mainline are still stuck in a review. The latest plan is less bullish about the immediate prospects for the other major route improvements that the government had heralded in its first version of its ten-year plan. The SRA has thought through how it wishes to amalgamate many of the franchises into stronger regional single company units. This is all part of its process to try and get more control and direction over the industry. It is very reminiscent of the decisions taken by the government in 1914 that ushered in a very long period of decline in railway usage.

What are railways good at?

The British railway network is trying to do at least four rather different things, often using the same track and signalling systems. Firstly, there is the commuter passenger railway. This is most important into the Greater London area and back again at morning and evening peaks. There are also important commuter railways into other big cities like Manchester and Birmingham. These railways require relatively slow trains to carry a large number of people short distances with frequent stops to pick up and put down the passengers. Secondly, there is the inter-city railway carrying far fewer people at far higher speeds over longer distances. The principal routes include the East Coast route from London to Edinburgh and the West Coast route from London to Glasgow. London/Leeds, London/Birmingham and London/Manchester are important routes in this network. Thirdly, there is the cross-country railway attempting to provide slower links than inter-city between provincial towns and cities. Fourthly, there is the freight railway, routing heavy goods from manufacturers to ports or from ports to warehouses or routing intermediate goods between the main industrial centres.

Inter-city

These different types of service impose rather different strains and requirements upon the railway. If you wish to run successful high-speed inter-city services it is best to have dedicated track. Running speeds are greatly increased if there are few stops, if the track bed is as flat as possible and if there are few or no curves. The Japanese have shown how Bullet trains can be run very successfully between major conurbations. They have the enormous advantage that the main settlements are in a fairly straight line along the coastal plain allowing the construction of remarkably flat and straight track for most of the journey, which permits very high speed. The more curves and gradients that are introduced the more problems there will be. Maintenance costs escalate geometrically with more curves and slopes as high-speed trains impose proportionately much greater strains on curved and sloping track. It is not easy to run fast successful inter-city services if you have to share the track with stopping commuter or cross-country services. Very careful timetabling is needed to make sure that the express is not held up at any point by slower moving trains.

Freight

The freight railway places a different kind of strain on the track owing to the very heavy weights through each axle. Freight trains tend to run very slowly. They are most economic if they are very long, very heavy and do not stop for long distances. In the USA, straight, flat tracks over the plains and prairies are very good for freight traffic. Trains of a mile long or more can be constructed and once the momentum has been achieved by slow acceleration from the point of departure they are then very fuel efficient and can journey very long distances without interruption, largely under their own momentum. It is not so easy if freight trains have to regularly be brought to a halt or slowed down to accommodate other traffic sharing the track or intersecting it.

The idea of a railway is to reduce the friction by running steel on steel. In its origins it was designed to make it easier for horses, donkeys and mules to drag heavy coal trucks out of the mine. The intention was to reduce the friction as much as possible so that the animals could pull as much weight as possible for their exertions. People soon gave up the idea of running steel or iron wheels on motor vehicles preferring rubber for the ride quality and for the adhesion it gave to increase the stability and improve braking distances.

Commuter railways

We should ask ourselves whether the current steel on steel technology is the best one for running a commuter railway. Every autumn we have problems with delays owing to leaves on the line. This has led the railways into a slash and burn policy, seeking to remove trees, hedges and shrubs which grow in profusion to screen the edge of the railway from land all along the track. Many residents living near railway lines have been dismayed by the demolition of the green barrier which offers some noise protection and visual screening. Environmentalists have been upset, as important habitats for wildlife have been scythed down. Despite all this, tracks do not remain leaf-free during the autumn and steel wheels slip and slide on leaf-encrusted track. In the winter, snow and ice can cause similar havoc, reducing the rather poor traction of a steel wheel.

On a modern railway, steel on steel makes a lot of sense for long-distance freight and for high-speed expresses. It does not make a great deal of sense for trains running commuter services where they have to regularly accelerate and decelerate requiring friction and traction as they move from station to station. It is time the railway industry examined new materials for its wheels that would solve the adhesion problem once and for all. If braking times and distances could be reduced then the number of trains that could use any given section of track during the morning and evening peak could be increased. If we look at the congested roads during the rush hour we can see that cars, vans, buses and lorries travel almost bumper to bumper, relatively safe in the knowledge that they can usually brake in good time to avoid contact with the vehicle in front. If, however, we examine the use of the railway we see the need for segregation of trains by a distance of more than one mile. As a general rule, by the time a driver can see something on the track that he needs to avoid, it is too late to stop to avoid it.

A mixed railway

Planning the use of the network and planning its maintenance is greatly complicated by mixing all these different modes of traffic on the same track. Track wear and tear is greatly increased by combining high speed and freight. Safe segregation of trains is made more difficult if trains of varying speeds and weights are mixed on the same line and if use of the line is at or near capacity. The government and the Strategic Rail Authority seem unlikely to be able to remove the blockages and capacity constraints on the network more quickly. As a result they are going to be faced with making some more invidious choices about the priorities for the use of our ageing and restricted rail system.

Most commentators, as well as the SRA and the government in its honest moments, agree that the network is now at or near capacity in many respects. Most agree that if we wish to sustain the phenomenal growth in train usage that we saw in the first five years after privatisation it will be necessary to increase capacity quickly and substantially.

Analysis of the usage patterns of the railways shows that the two most effective uses for trains in our congested island are for commuter passengers and freight. Our motorways and trunk roads are at their most congested in the morning and evening peaks of working days. People are most inclined to switch to train usage where their car journeys are most delayed and where there are frequent and regular services available on the trains. This should be easiest to achieve for commuters into and out of the main centres of work during the working week. London has shown that it is possible to move a high proportion of the workforce in the morning and evening by train although the current standards of the service leave a lot to be desired.

Maglev technology

The Japanese also believe that technology needs to be changed for fast train services. Steel wheels on flat, straight steel tracks are fine for achieving running speeds of up to 200 miles per hour. This still does not make the train competitive with the plane in terms of journey time if the person wishes to travel several hundred miles. A train is clearly competitive in terms of time when travelling the 130 miles from London to Birmingham, given the time it takes to check in and get off the plane. It is not competitive with the plane between London and Edinburgh where the actual flight takes less than an hour.

The Japanese have developed a new technology called Maglev.

In the Maglev system the train is lifted off the track by super-conducting magnets and driven forward by a linear motor. In 1987 the Japanese achieved running speeds of 400 kilometres per hour and in 1990 their government turned it into a nationally funded project. In 1997 they opened a new test line in the Yamanashi prefecture. On 12 December 1997 they achieved 531 kilometres per hour, topping that at 550 kilometres per hour on 24 December. On 14 April 1999 they achieved a maximum speed of 552 kilometres per hour with a five-car train set. A Maglev train runs along a guideway. On board, super-conducting magnets with an opposite force provide the forward propulsion on the newer versions of these Maglev vehicles. The German consortium of Siemens, Thyssen Krupp and Adtranz are also developing a magnetic levitation technology.

The United Kingdom is trying to produce tilting trains to deal with the problem of too many curves for high-speed operation. These have proved problematic and can only raise the running speeds by a relatively modest amount. Many people are coming to the conclusion that in order to have high-speed inter-city trains in Britain new track is required. Part of the problem over the escalation of costs for the West Coast Mainline is just this, that in order to achieve a twenty-five mile per hour increase in average running speed for an express they are effectively having to create a new track which is straighter and flatter. Maybe we should be asking ourselves if we want very fast surface travel over the longer distances between centres like London, Edinburgh and Glasgow. We should consider leap-frogging when the new technology is perfected and building a dedicated guideway for a very fast train.

Freight and the environment
Developing the freight railway provides us with the biggest scope for environmental gains. If the commuter railway is a congestion buster the freight railway would be the quickest way of removing a large number of heavily polluting large vehicles. It would also greatly improve the traffic flows on the road if we could remove many heavy lorries. In the era of nationalisation rail freight slumped. One of the main reasons for this was that in the later years the nationalised industry was not interested in single wagon business. If you wished to be a customer of rail freight you had to have a trainload of traffic on a regular basis. The leading oil companies, the leading motorcar manufacturers, the big aggregates businesses, British Steel as it then was and the cement manufacturers could make or generate enough products at a single

site to justify whole train traffic. Most British businesses were ruled out of rail freight because they simply did not have the volumes. A dominant use of the railway for freight was in carrying coal and coke from the coalmines to the power stations and the steelworks. Whilst this was useful, it meant that rail freight slumped to a far smaller proportion of total goods moved in Britain than in the continental countries.

One of the advantages of privatisation was that the railways became interested again in single wagon business. It is a job of the railway to assemble single wagon business from a number of different industrial customers and create trainloads that can be transported around the country. Over the declining years of nationalisation business had got out of the habit of locating itself near to principal rail routes. Property specialists are now keen to locate industrial parks and new industrial premises close to motorway junctions. They recognise that the predominant means of travel for the raw materials and goods has become the lorry. Now that the railways are interested again in medium sized consignments of freight we need to reintroduce the rail option into our planning process. All too many industrial parks are now too far away from a main railway line to make it easy or feasible to introduce spur or branch lines to make rail freight easy from the place of manufacture. Where we are designing new industrial plants and new industrial parks we should, wherever possible, try to have a rail freight option. If you visit Trafford Park in Manchester, once one of Europe's largest industrial parks in the inter-war years, you will see that it is criss-crossed with branch lines and sidings as it was originally designed to be firmly linked to the main rail network. If you visit more modern industrial parks they tend to lie along the routes of the main motorways like the M4 or adjacent to big airports like Heathrow and Manchester.

The future

The government's current plans for attracting private capital into the railway industry have been badly damaged by the bankruptcy of Railtrack, foolishly brought on by a government minister. The original 'ten year plan' was not ambitious enough. The amounts of private capital envisaged were never going to be enough to modernise and expand the railways sufficiently. The target of increasing rail capacity by a half was not big enough to make a large impact on the UK's travel problems. When the railway starts with only a 7% market share, an increase of 50% will only take care of a couple of year's overall growth in travel demands. It will not allow a major switch from motorcars and lorries to trains. Now the 'ten year plan' is delayed and damaged. It will take a bold new initiative to put the railways back properly into the private sector.

Histories show that Britain's railways grew and flourished with private enterprise and private capital and have declined under government regulation and control throughout most of the twentieth century. It will not be possible to sustain a railway trying to do all things for all men. We should concentrate on getting the freight and commuter railways right. They should take most of the money. We need big increases in the capacity of both and better links to the road system to allow people and goods to get to and from the trains. This will require the return of Railtrack to the private sector, removing Railtrack's monopoly so that others can build and own track as well. It will also require a new enthusiasm for privatisation to raise the huge sums required. The existing train companies should have their franchises renewed so they can get on with the equally important task of investing in new rolling stock, which will also be needed to attract people back to the trains.

The government and the Rail Regulator have decided they would like to rationalise the private railway industry, creating just one train operating company into each major London terminus. This will delay the provision of private capital for much needed new rolling stock and locomotives, and cause considerable uncertainty in the industry. It is difficult to see what benefits will occur. At the moment some travellers have a choice of train company to carry out their journey. This can be very valuable if, for example, one of the train companies on their line experiences industrial relations or technical problems. The customer has a choice and can switch to the other operator. Concentration on just one company will expose more travellers to risk of delay or shut down of the service. It is another example of regulatory intervention damaging the prospects of growth in the industry.

We need a new vision. There needs to be more choice, private capital and privatisation, not less. The government has now done a deal with the shareholders of Railtrack, to lift the threat of legal action. It will speed up returning Railtrack to the private sector. Until that is accomplished the plans for new investment will remain delayed or cancelled. The idea that it can be run by a 'not for profit' company limited by guarantee is not a good one. The danger is that the taxpayer will have to guarantee all the capital. The business will not be able to build up reserves, and private investors will want generous interest payments, underwritten by the government, if they cannot share in the profits. The government has acknowledged that the new Railtrack will not have a big enough balance sheet or enough financial supporters to be able to build the lines and modernise long sections of track. It plans to do these through so-called 'special purpose vehicles', more public private partnership companies that will require substantial taxpayer guarantees to get off the ground. The irony is that Labour will end up with a railway that is in practice a pensioner of the state, but without it being fully in public ownership. It will raise money at considerable cost, and will split the network under different managements as a result of the financing problem. It would be cheaper to renationalise it and bring it back under state planning completely, but far cheaper and better to privatise it properly and allow a 'for-profit' company to raise the money needed to modernise the network. On the railways the Third Way is the dearest, and the one that entails most delay.

Third Way on the railways so far has meant bankruptcy for Railtrack, and threats and delays for the train operating companies. The new Third Way company, Network Rail, will find it difficult to pick up the pieces. It will in practice be dependent on public money. Not for profit means no dividends. The uncertain financial background will mean leaders will want government guarantees. It will turn out to be a very expensive way of running a public monopoly. The government's interference will be at one remove, adding to the uncertainties and difficulties. Third Way railways will end up needing new backing, as too much is demanded of too little.

Chapter six

THE UNDERGROUND –
MORE THIRD WORLD THAN THIRD WAY

TRANSPORT PATTERNS IN LONDON are different from the rest of the country owing to the density of population in the capital. In 2000, 7.3 million people lived in the Greater London area whilst the total number of people employed increased to 4.5 million.

On a typical weekday, around 1.1 million people enter central London between 7.00am and 10.00am and are very dependent on public transport. Many Londoners do not choose to own a car, with 37% of households in Greater London not having a car or van, compared with 27% for the country as a whole. Far fewer households in Greater London have two or more cars than in the richer parts of the country outside the capital. These figures do not only reflect pockets of poverty within the London area but also the conscious decisions of some of the most affluent people in the country to rely on taxis, chauffeur cars and public transport rather than owning a vehicle of their own. Many houses in central London have no garage and little or no parking space on the street outside. Many houses have no dedicated parking of any kind, which makes owning a car a nuisance especially when returning home to discover the neighbours have taken the parking place.

Motorists in London suffer more than anywhere else in the country owing to a combination of very limited road space for good historical and architectural reasons, draconian traffic management measures, restrictions on parking and on use of the roads. Average traffic speeds are now around ten miles per hour. During the period between 2000 and 2001, over four million penalty charge notices were issued by London boroughs for parking offences, of which the inner London boroughs accounted for two thirds. Average incomes in London are over a fifth higher than the rest of the United Kingdom but Londoners tend to travel less far than people outside the city owing to the relatively short distances they need to go. The table beneath shows the number of miles travelled each year by Londoners compared with the Great Britain average and the percentages by different means of travel.

Mode of Travel	London		Great Britain	
Bus and coach	390 miles	7.1%	345 miles	5.0%
London Underground	369 miles	6.8%	57 miles	0.9%
National Rail	586 miles	10.6%	371 miles	5.4%
Taxi/Minicab	83 miles	1.6%	62 miles	0.9%
Car and van	3,598 miles	66.0%	5,573 miles	81.5%
Motorcycle	65 miles	1.2%	30 miles	0.4%
Bicycle	38 miles	0.7%	38 miles	0.5%
Walking	225 miles	4.0%	186 miles	2.7%
Other	108 miles	2.0%	180 miles	2.7%
All modes	**Total** 5,462 miles	100%	**Total** 6,843 miles	100%

Source: Transport Statistics for London 2001 issued by Transport for London 2001

If we look at the main means of getting to work the figures also reveal a very different position for London from the rest of Britain with a strikingly different set of figures for the narrow central London area.

Area of Workplace			
	Central London	All London	Great Britain
Car and van	13%	43%	70%
Motorcycle	1%	1%	1%
Bicycle	2%	2%	3%
Bus and coach	9%	10%	8%
National Rail	39%	18%	5%
London Underground	32%	17%	2%
Walking	4%	9%	11%
Total	100%	100%	100%

Source: Transport Statistics for London 2001 issued by Transport for London 2001

Please note that these tables are reproduced from original sources and we are therefore not responsible for any inaccuracies.

As these figures reveal, in the most highly congested and densely packed metropolitan area in Britain, there is a sufficient volume of people to install a mass transit system to handle the bulk of the peak travel. This only works in a very narrow central area. The inner London figures are less dramatic than just central London and once the figures of the whole of London are used, the pattern is getting rather more like the country as a whole. In the outer-lying suburban areas of the Greater London area there simply is not the same density. As a result people are much further from tube stations and bus stops. Service frequency and access are often poor. Faced with a more limited public sector transport choice, people turn much more to the car for their travel.

Why do people use the tube and the bus in central London, particularly for their journey to work? In most cases people have no option. There is far too little available road space for anything more than a small fraction of the people wishing to travel to work in central London. Most people have no access to parking at their journey's end and recognise that they need a public transport alternative. In the central area the public transport alternative is as good as you get in the United Kingdom and is markedly better than practically anywhere else. Although the tube and bus service has its frustrations, with too many delays, cancellations and breakdowns, there is considerable choice with densely packed tube routes in the central area allowing some flexibility of route planning should lines or trains fail. In the peak periods service frequency is quite high, particularly on the most congested central lines and bus routes.

Many people using the tube or bus service would like it to be a lot better and use it because they have no real alternative. The government would say that the London experience shows that if you make it difficult enough for people to use their cars they will switch to public transport. The public would say that there would be no chance of replicating the high volume of public transport service in central London in most other places in the country and that therefore one must treat the London experience as something very different.

The London Underground

The London Underground is in a state of great uncertainty. Massive reorganisation of the ownership structure is underway with the transfer of responsibilities from the Secretary of State for Transport to Transport for London. On 1 April 2000, London Transport transferred the majority of its property and operational assets to three subsidiaries: London Underground, London Bus Services and Transport Trading in preparation for the creation of Transport for London. On 3 July 2000, Transport Trading, London Bus Services and Victoria Coach Station transferred to Transport for London leaving London Underground with three new subsidiaries to handle engineering owned by London Transport.

London Transport is now something of a dinosaur. Practically all the other large, nationalised corporations of the post-war period have been subjected to competition and transferred to the private sector. London Underground remains with a monopoly over all underground train travel owning track, trains, signals and property assets under a single, unified command answerable to the government of London and the National government. The intention is that London Underground should be answerable to Transport for London, the Mayor and the Greater London Assembly. In practice the Underground has been caught in a push-me-pull-me between the National government and the new London government over how it should be organised for the future.

In the meantime the story of London Underground is a very typical nationalised industry story. The system is under considerable financial pressure, short of funds to invest and modernise in the way that it would like. It is chronically short of capacity, particularly at peak times in the central area but is unable to solve the capacity problem claiming that this will require substantial investment and very long-term projects. The standard of service is not good, with many passengers complaining about delays, cancellations, dirty trains, dirty stations and a lack of customer care. In recent years labour relations have been poor with sporadic strikes and stoppages reflecting staff unhappiness about the way they are directed and about terms and conditions of employment.

In the year to 31 March 2001, London Underground earned £1,223 million from its customers, mainly through fares for train travel. After allowing for depreciation, but before grant, it lost £293.4 million. A public sector monopoly which has been given permission for some substantial real fare increases over the last thirty years still manages to make losses. This is due to a combination of a lack of imagination in obtaining more revenue from its passengers through better service, and difficulty in controlling its costs owing to poor labour relations and the manning efficiencies that have to be built into the system.

The balance sheets show an even more extraordinary picture. The current value of the London Underground system is given in the official Report and Accounts as a little under £3,000 million. Until recently the assets were valued at a little over £8,000 million but the government has decided, with its auditors, to write off £5,370 million of the capital to reflect a proper depreciation charge on old assets.

The government and their auditors may well be realistic in saying the total value of the whole tube system is only £2,923.7 million. Certainly, in its current shape, anyone thinking of taking it over would be well aware that, whilst there is considerable scope to grow the revenues, there are many liabilities and a substantial requirement for funds to improve and modernise. The assets have already been written down as part of the preparatory work for the public private partnership. Anyone contemplating entering complex long-term business relationships with London

Underground would want to know that there had been a realistic assessment of the current state of the track, signals and trains and a full realisation by the present owners, the National and London governments, that a great deal needs to be done to improve the system.

The accounts of London Underground, in their new slimmed down form, make an important point that became apparent when privatising other great networks like the telephone system. We spend a great deal of our time and energy debating what to do with these priceless national assets but, on further inspection, discover they are in a pretty poor state and that what matters is how we spend new money on completely transforming them.

The really valuable thing in London Underground's ownership is the series of tunnels underground. It would cost many billions to cut similar tunnels today. However, I think we have to regard the tunnels themselves as a sunk cost, long since written off. The tunnels and the routes they represent may well in effect have to be given to whoever is going to operate the underground system successfully. There is far less value in the signalling systems, the track and the train sets operating over it. Much of this is old and in need of renewal. The technology itself is old fashioned. It is only possible to run thirty-two trains an hour on the Central Line when passenger demand would require rather more at peak periods. The operator needs to have decent segregation to allow for the poor braking times and distances even at the relatively slow speeds operated on the Central Line in the congested middle section. The Paris Metro on some of its lines, faced with problems of steeper gradients, opted for rubber tyres to provide more grip and adhesion. This does allow better acceleration and better braking, offering more traction than steel wheels on steel rails. The signalling systems also impose limitations on the number of trains that can be run safely in any given hour and are themselves unreliable, often breaking down and causing delays. The more modern trains on the new Jubilee Line provide higher standards of passenger comfort but have not been without teething problems. All too many train sets on the Underground system have no air-conditioning, which makes the travel experience particularly unpleasant on hot days in the summer.

In the last decade there has been a 25% increase in Underground usage. The directors themselves state that this has increased "strain on the ageing network and further emphasises the need for sustained and substantial investment in the system". Only 91.6% of services operated in the last year ran to time, leading the board to conclude, "reliability in some areas has fallen below acceptable levels". The state of the track now necessitates closures from time to time. In summer 2000, it was necessary to close the Victoria Line between Victoria and Brixton for three weeks to replace worn out rails. The District Line from Earls Court to High Street Kensington also had to be closed for strengthening work to be carried out to the tunnel.

During the 1990's, substantial investment was going into the tube, primarily to build the Jubilee Line extension. The amount of investment going in has now plummeted. In 1999 to 2000, expenditure was running at £944 million whereas 2000 to 2001 saw it fall by more than two thirds to £300 million. There are no major projects currently underway.

The proposed public private partnership

The new government elected in 1997 decided that it did not wish to privatise the tube but it did wish to bring in substantial sums of private capital. The government was constantly promising rapid progress. Tube capital expenditure was depressed compared with the levels under the previous government. The government promised much more money from the PPP. Five years on and at last we know the shape of the planned public private partnership. We also know that it is producing a big row between the Mayor with Transport for London on the one hand, and London Underground and the government on the other. It is an excellent example of the crosscurrents and conflicts inherent in trying to find a third way between a privatised industry on the one hand and a wholly state-run and state-financed industry on the other.

The government hoped that developing a public private partnership would allow substantial tube investment expenditure to be financed off the government's balance sheet at no direct cost to the tax payer while at the same time reassuring the Labour left and the trade unions that the business itself was not being fully privatised. The government has found that it has critics ranged strongly on both sides.

Privatisers say that the PPP system creates enormous muddle and confusion and is the equivalent of government borrowing in the long run but at much greater cost. People on the left point out that the private sector companies' involvement would give considerable freedom to change the manpower and employment arrangements of the staff who maintain and expand the track. For them it is too similar to privatisation, which they fear and dislike.

The government's plans propose splitting the running and owning of the trains from running, owning and maintaining the track and signalling system. It caught many commentators by surprise when the government decided that the train sets and the provision of train services should remain a public sector activity. This would be organised under the loose control of Transport for London acting through London Underground management whilst the provision of track would be contracted out to three different private groups. The government established an elaborate bidding process that went on for many months. They divided the network into three different sections, splitting the overground and sub-surface into one contract and dividing the deep tube system into two. The bidding process turned out to be long, with frequent modifications from both sides, the government's and the bidding parties'. The end result is a scheme with an extremely complicated contractual relationship stretching over a possible thirty years for each bidder. The pricing is only settled for the first seven and a half years and there is a certain vagueness about what has to be achieved and how it will be paid for especially after the seven and a half year point in the thirty-year contracts.

Transport for London's critique of the tube PPP

Transport for London and the Mayor have been strong critics of the whole idea. During the electoral contest for Mayor, Ken Livingstone centred much of his campaign on the proposition that the tube should remain a service organised and provided by the public sector. He claims that his opposition to the PPP struck a chord with the public and was one of the main reasons why he won. Nonetheless, the government decided that it had an electoral mandate to push through the PPP and was keen to do so before the Underground system fell completely under the control of the Mayor and Transport for London. As a result court actions were undertaken, with the Mayor and TfL extremely unhappy about the proposals.

TfL record their objections to the PPP in the following terms: "in sum: the PPP path leads to the transfer of ownership and control of the infrastructure comprising London Underground to the private sector, and leaves to the private sector virtually all decision making authority over what investments will be made and when. In the first seven and a half years of the contract, London Underground will pay the private sector approximately £1 billion per year (subject to the infraco's right to reopen the price if its initial pricing assumptions prove to be too low) in return for a general promise to maintain and upgrade the tube infrastructure, a fee which is calculated based on investment proposals that the private sector is largely free to abandon or modify. For later years, the amount to be paid to the private sector is not established (a third party arbiter is to set that pricing if the parties cannot agree) and even the private financing of capital investment, the very purpose of a PPP arrangement, is not guaranteed. Yet London Underground will not be free to deviate from the thirty-year path". The detailed critique of the PPP extends over a further seven pages in their February 2002 document. They are critical of the failure of the contracts to define what London Underground gets for the money it is paying. They point out that there are complex mathematical models to determine whether to pay bonuses or not to the contractors and illustrate that however badly the contractors perform at least 90% of the £1 billion per year has to be paid. Furthermore, they point out that bonuses will be paid to the private sector even if performance deteriorates by up to 5% compared with current performance. If the infracos get in financial trouble or default or do damage to the rest of London Underground, there is no recourse by TfL and the taxpayers to the people and companies that might stand behind them. There is no guarantee that any money will be provided after the first seven and half years.

If the infracos incur costs that exceed the estimates by an average of almost £27 million per year and can sustain the argument that the overruns are reasonable they must be paid in full for these overruns. The infracos have considerable scope to decide how to spend the money they are granted and will have monopoly power over planned major projects in the future if London Underground seeks to implement them. If a private sector infraco defaults it has a one-year period to try to find a buyer to recover the value of its investment. If no buyer can be found London Underground Limited has to make default payments to the very private sector parties who breached the contract in the first place to protect private sector lenders. If LUL defaults or wishes to default it has to pay thirty-year profits to the infracos. At the end of the thirty-year period London Underground is expected to assume whatever debt has been placed on the assets transferred to the private sector. Transport for London is also very critical of the safety arrangements and concludes that the project is not value for money.

The government believes these claims are exaggerated and is satisfied that the tube project is a good one. It has relied heavily upon a study undertaken for it by Ernst & Young to determine whether the PPP was better value for money than state funding. Their conclusion is quite masterful. They state "overall the methodology adopted for assessing the value for money by London Underground has been robust and appropriate: and London Underground's recommendation that the PPP proposals deliver value for money is a subjective one which is supported by its analysis." The government seizes on this saying that effectively Ernst & Young has endorsed the method of analysis of London Underground and has said that it is indeed value for money to go for the PPP. Critics point out that Ernst & Young has very carefully distanced itself. The firm has not said that they believe that it would definitely be value for money. They have said that London Underground has adopted a perfectly sensible method but have had to make subjective judgements along the way. They leave it for individual readers of the London Underground scheme and their analysis to make their own minds up on whether the scheme is value for money. Ernst & Young do give certain hints to their readers about what they should be asking themselves. For example, they point out that although the contract term is thirty years there are periodic reviews of the terms beginning at the seven and a half year review. This warns readers to realise that it is quite impossible to judge whether it will be value for money over the whole thirty years or not because we have no idea what it will cost. Secondly, they point out "risk transfer is complex and subject to various sharing and limitation procedures" which means that one would need a very complicated model and all sorts of assumptions about how the risks might work out in order to come to a balanced judgement. They remind readers that the whole scheme is based on the assumption that the private sector option will perform better than the public and point out that the valuation is of a very long time period that greatly increases the hazards of getting it right.

One of the crucial points to understand about the assessment is this question of different expected levels of performance from the public and private sector options. The so-called 'social cost adjustments' take into account their judgment of increased or decreased journey times and service levels under the different schemes. The public sector option has its cost increased by 9% and the private sector option its cost decreased by 5% to allow for the assumed better performance of the private sector. This is the equivalent of a £2,100 million advantage to the private sector scheme.

It is quite likely that the private sector option will perform better than the public but it is important when making the assessment to understand that we are comparing apples and pears and having to quantify rather different proposals in cash terms. If comparison is made simply based on cash figures, without the social adjustments to provide the overall value figures, the contrast between a public sector scheme and a PPP is much less marked. There is no guarantee that a PPP will work like a free enterprise company, as it is a very different animal with strong public sector involvement.

Ernst & Young stress that the very complicated risk transfers involved in the contracts are new. They state: "the contract structure is unique, inevitably meaning that it has not been proven in a commercial environment…if the contract structure, in particular the risk transfer and review mechanisms, does not function effectively, either through poor design or operation, then there is a risk that value for money could be eroded". They also point out that London Underground has very limited commercial leverage if things go wrong because of its potential liability in the event of terminating the arrangements.

What are the options for the tube?

There are four major options for the future of London Underground. Two were in serious discussion during 2001 and the first half of 2002. The first is the government's PPP scheme as outlined above. The second is Transport for London's scheme under the guidance of the Mayor. The third is a pure public sector option, continuing with a nationalised, publicly provided, integrated monopoly railway under overall political direction and day-to-day executive management control, entirely financed by passengers and taxpayers. The fourth would be a proper privatisation, perhaps along the lines of the Londoner's Tube scheme which the Conservative party adopted for a time under William Hague.

Transport for London's scheme

Transport for London believe that they must have unified management control over the system and all private sector contractors servicing it. TfL believe there needs to be a sharp increase in investment compared with the levels of the last couple of years, proposing a figure of around £850 million a year subject to a proper investigation of the state of the infrastructure. They are against any real increases in train fares and believe that the government should provide the Underground with a stable level of annual grants. They want the Greater London Authority to use its authority to raise additional revenues to provide additional finance for the system. They are happy to have some private sector contractors working but believe they should be more strictly limited in what they can do and directly under the control of Transport for London.

TfL wish to raise the money from a variety of sources. Firstly, there are the operating revenues of the Underground. Secondly, they want grants from the government. Thirdly, they would like to offer long-term highly rated public bonds secured on the revenues of London Underground itself. Fourthly, they would look to private contractors to produce equity contributions for the construction or rehabilitation of specific assets and for maintenance projects.

TfL and its Commissioner, Mr Bob Kiley, lay great stress on the need to have a proper engineering assessment to work out what is required to improve the state of the existing assets. They have much less to say on the provision of new facilities. They wish to use the private sector to improve and furnish the right kind of infrastructure. Their idea is to ring-fence certain contracts, rewarding the contractor if he does the job properly but making him liable for all of the costs that result from any failure. They would insist that any business undertaking one of these contracts offer financial guarantees. They sum up their idea in the sentence "the Mayor and Transport for London would seek to combine the best features of public sector oversight and management with the competitive drive of the private sector to build, rebuild and refurbish the underground in fifteen years". They are keen to improve performance, seeking to reduce waiting times, delays, unreliability of escalators, overcrowding, providing better information and creating a sense of greater security. Analysis undertaken so far illustrates that train, signal and track failures are very heavily concentrated on certain lines. By far the worst is the Piccadilly Line with more than 1,400 cancellations of trains between December 1999 and November 2000, in the peak period. More than 1,200 of these train failures resulted from the failure of trains themselves. The next biggest cause or difficulty was signal failure. The Central Line is the second worst line with over 800 peak period train cancellations in the same year, with the vast majority as a result of faulty trains. The third worst performing line is the District Line with just under 600 cancellations, mostly because of track failure. The Metropolitan and Northern Lines were also poor performers, their main problem being train failures.

Transport for London points out that under the PPP proposals several of the line upgrades are offered as late as 2020, meaning continuing misery for many years to come. The analysis shows that a relatively modest expenditure of money on new train sets for the Piccadilly, Central, Northern and Metropolitan Lines could have a dramatic impact upon the overall reliability of the system assuming they chose to buy trains which worked. Track renewal on the District and the Hammersmith and City Lines would also make an important contribution to reliability. Signalling is worst on the Piccadilly, Metropolitan, District and Hammersmith and City Lines and would also benefit from some attention.

Transport for London does recognise, however, that in the longer term overcrowding will get worse unless there is a major expansion of capacity. In 1981 and 1982, the Underground handled 541 million passenger journeys whilst during the period 2000 to 2001 the figure had almost doubled to 970 million causing considerable overcrowding on several lines at busy times of the day. The Mayor proposes rehabilitation and modernisation of the existing system in the first instance. However, he recognises that major new rail projects will be needed and suggests some examination of extending the East London Line, extending the line north to Dalston where it will connect with the North London Line, and then south to connect with the National Rail Network in south London. He suggests that we need Crossrail, a high capacity east/west rail link joining the city to Heathrow. He would also like the Hackney/South West Line to connect between Victoria and Dalston via Piccadilly Circus and Tottenham Court Road. The Mayor does not propose starting work on construction of the Hackney South West Line, the main Underground project, until 2011, with the opening delayed until 2015.

Transport for London is also reluctant to see facilities made available for motorists to park and ride at tube stations, except at the most outlying stations. Indeed, the strategy document includes proposals to make on-street parking near tube stations more difficult. There are policies to promote better access for pedestrians and cyclists and to try to improve facilities for the disabled.

What then should we make of this project? It is undoubtedly more straightforward than the government's plan but it is not without its drawbacks. The biggest hurdle the Mayor and Transport for London have to leap is the government's unwillingness to co-operate in any way with this plan. The Treasury is not persuaded that London Underground Bonds issued against the security of the revenues is sufficiently distanced from public sector finance. As the assets remain owned and managed in the public sector there would of course be recourse by city financiers should something go wrong to the taxpayer. It would not be possible to ring-fence it. There is also undoubtedly an animus in the disagreement. The Labour government bitterly opposed Ken Livingstone's attempt to become Mayor and forced him to run as an Independent. Ken Livingstone is a shrewd politician who knows that the government is going through a long period of unpopularity and who sees an opportunity to exploit this by pursuing a different line on the Underground to that of the Transport Secretary and Prime Minister. Now that the Mayor's court action against London Underground and the government has failed, it is difficult to see the dispute being patched up easily. It is also very likely that ideas coming from the Mayor and Mr Kiley will now be received particularly badly by the Transport Department.

There are also some weaknesses in the plans. The money is likely to be more limited than TfL and the Mayor would like. They wish to lower fares or keep fares down at the same time as increasing spending. There is only so much money that the City would be prepared to advance secured against the revenues without an explicit government guarantee. As soon as the government guarantee is given we are back to the same problem that no British government is ever likely to afford a high enough priority to the tube to give it the very large sums, over a sustained period, that it will need for modernisation and expansion.

Nor would the idea of contracting out to the private sector be entirely free of risk and difficulty. Mr Kiley and Transport for London have been very shrewd in mounting a strong critique of the government's public private partnership contracts. They are right, that they are very complex, unproven, and leave a large number of loopholes for the private sector to avoid risk or responsibility when certain things go wrong. Mr Kiley assumes that it will be relatively easy to correct all these faults in the type of contracts he is proposing. However, given what he says about the current state of the assets, the private sector is going to be very wary of entering binding contractual obligations to maintain and improve assets without a guarantee about their current state and an understanding of possible remedial costs. It is difficult for Mr Kiley to have it both ways in practice. It may be a good debating ploy to claim that the existing state of the assets is terrible and, at the same time, claim that there are private contractors out there who would love to bind themselves to remedying all those defects for a modest price with full financial guarantees backing them. Life is rarely that easy since the private sector would want to reduce its risk and to have certain warranties from London Underground before entering such binding contractual arrangements. Of course, it would be possible for London Underground to let a series of contracts to improve track and signals to a given specification, procuring the steel, the equipment and the engineering works from the private sector. If the public sector wishes to go further, as TfL implies, to transfer ownership of portions of the track and responsibility for making it available under the general management control of Transport for London, things will get far more complicated and probably more expensive. The Kiley scheme only appears better than the PPP for the time being because the PPP is the scheme that the government intends to implement and most critical attention has been turned on that. Should the roles ever be reversed, and Transport for London get the upper hand over which scheme is going to be implemented, more of the criticism will turn to the TfL scheme. The government might well be able to mount a critique of that in a similar vein to the one mounted by TfL before the PPP.

A nationalised tube owned and managed in the public sector
I never thought I would be an advocate of a nationalised industry under public control but if I had to choose between the existing way of owning and running the Tube and the PPP and TfL models, I think I would rather keep it as it is. At least then more radical proposals for the future would not be ruled out, and at least we would not have to go through a very expensive and drawn out learning curve as we discovered whether the private sector contractors operating under PPP or TfL rules were, in practice, a good idea. The problems with the public sector monopoly approach are well known. They dogged many British nationalised industries in the post-war period up to privatisation. They are kept short of public money for investment, they find it difficult to control costs and raise efficiency, and all but impossible to motivate their workforce effectively. They become prey to inefficient working practices and the absence of share incentive or proper bonus schemes can produce a negative approach. Most of these public monopolies entrust customer contact to the lowest paid and often the worst motivated of all the staff employed. Staff morale is often low as a result of the conditions and terms of employment, and staff turnover high. None of this is conducive to successful organisation.

Were the tube to stay in the public sector following an inconclusive battle between the TfL plans and government's plans it would undoubtedly need more money and better management. It will need a similar level of investment funding to that which it enjoyed throughout much of the 1990's when it was constructing the Jubilee Line. The collapse in investment and grant funding following the termination of the Jubilee Line construction has left the tube very short of money to renovate existing assets, let alone to expand the size of the network.

Good public sector managers would begin from the analysis of current weaknesses and remedy the malfunctioning train sets, the defective track and failing signals on those lines where the problems are most acute. Attention should then be turned as quickly as possible to raising the capacity on the most popular lines which would require tackling signalling and braking systems in order to run more trains on the existing, fairly congested, network. A successful management would also persuade the government of the day to finance at least one major project, probably the Hackney/Chelsea Line, preferably learning from the cost overruns and difficulties encountered in the construction of the Jubilee extension.

This model is clearly the simplest and involves the least re-organisation. It has one overwhelming defect. There is no competitive element at all, meaning that all costs and service standards go unchallenged by the rigour of the market place. For this reason it could not be a long-term or permanent solution for anyone who really cares about raising the quality of service of the Underground.

The Londoner's Tube

Privatising the London Underground in the traditional offer for sale of a public monopoly would not be a good idea. I would not welcome a share issue in an integrated monopoly railway system in the hope that a new regulator would be able to balance fare rises against quality of service and make sure that safety and efficiency were taken into account. Whilst it would remove any financial strain from the government sector and might produce more money for capital investment, there would be considerable difficulties in policing the monopoly through a regulator. The government would always be open to monopolist pressure to give in on the scale of fare rises.

Far better would be to create something completely new, a Londoner's Tube. When I first developed the scheme the balance sheet of London Underground stated that the value of the assets was around £8,000 million. As we have seen, there have been massive write-downs recently, reducing the asset value to a little under

£3,000 million. This is despite the obvious hidden value of some excellent routes under some of the most expensive real estate in the world and reflects the liabilities that go with those routes: employee costs, safety risks and maintenance costs.

The first element in the Londoner's Tube is to introduce some competition. This would best be done in the congested and confined spaces of tube tunnels by splitting the London Underground system into four company ownerships; each company owning several complete lines, track, train, signals and stations. In the central area, in particular, there would be substantial choice as it is quite possible to select more than one line for carrying out many central area journeys. A fifth company called London Underground Limited would be the franchise holder. This company would be responsible for through ticketing and ticket sales and systems, for metro cards and discounted travel, the promotion of the London Underground as a whole, issuing tube maps and logos, and for promoting the construction of more tube capacity. This company would be financed by a very small overage or commission on turnover of the four major tube service providing companies who, in return, would get the benefits of the ticketing and promotional services of London Underground. The overage would be determined under a formula at the time of the original transaction. Receipts would rise as and when tube turnover and passenger numbers rose.

Shares in these five companies would be given to every Londoner and every season ticket holding commuter, using the tube system from wherever they may come in the country. Each individual voter in London and each individual season ticket holder, whether in London or from outside, would be able to apply for free shares. Evidence from free share issues to employees in previous privatisations illustrates that well over 90% of people are likely to apply for their shares. There should also be additional free shares for employees and there would be a further free distribution, to all those who had participated, of any shares that were unclaimed during the first offer.

Becoming a shareholder in the tube would entitle people to a discount on all tickets they bought provided they showed their shareholder's card which would be issued at the time of the share transfer. The shares could be freely traded on the London Stock Exchange but once a Londoner had sold his or her shares, he or she would cease to qualify for the ticket discounts on the tube. People would, in the usual way, be free to give or grant their shares under normal company law.

Once the shares have been issued, and a quote established on the London Stock Exchange, there would then be a Stock Exchange value for the tube system. It might be that the Stock Exchange decided that the current tube balance sheet undervalued it a little, given the great value and potential of the routes underground. Alternatively, the Stock Exchange might decide that there needed to be a discount to asset value, as in many companies, to reflect the uncertainties and the hidden costs. The important thing is that we would allow the market place to settle what is the current value of the tube. After a limited period of trading, to establish this value, the tube companies would then be required to issue a substantial pool of new equity to any individual or institution from Britain or overseas who wished to purchase the new shares. These would be offered at a small discount to the established market price of the existing shares. The aim would be to raise at least £2,000 million of new money for development of the tube system from the share issue.

Once this money had been raised the different tube companies would get their fair and specified proportions of it and would be better placed to carry out modernisation of the existing network with the cash. These companies would have the capacity to borrow at least £4,000 million additional capital given the relative stability of tube passenger revenues from the banking system and private market.

It would be the task of the governing authorities organising the sale of London Underground Limited (the franchise company), to secure money from these sources for the construction of two new lines. Any one of the existing four companies could offer to construct one of these new lines and the proportion of new shares issued would reflect its financing needs for that purpose. It would also be open to London Underground Limited to help a new company or an existing company in a different field to raise money for one or more of the new lines at the time of these transactions.

There would be certain requirements placed on the new companies before they were transferred from public to private ownership. The Mayor and Transport for London's list of improvements for the tube is fine in as far as it goes but there are some notable absences from the list. Firstly, there would be a requirement that air conditioning should be installed on all trains in the network by a specified date. People do expect a higher degree of comfort in the summer than they currently achieve on hot days. Secondly, plans should be drawn up to include much better car parking at or near more tube stations, especially in the outlying areas. If we wish to encourage many more people to leave the car and go by train it is most important that they have somewhere to park at the railhead. Thirdly, London Underground Limited would promote the development of property at stations, especially encouraging underground shopping malls at the most prestigious locations in the centre of London. Current shop rents and footfalls show that there is capacity for more good retail space in London. Shopping malls adjacent to leading underground stations like Oxford Circus would be especially attractive, providing all-weather, warm shopping areas with easy tube access and providing an addition to the London shopping experience that is very popular in countries like Canada.

This scheme is something completely different. It would offer ownership of the London Underground to Londoners and those who use it. It would offer them an incentive to remain as owners by giving them a discount on tube travel. This seems a better way of letting visitors pay more than a visitor's surcharge which is sometimes suggested. It might win people over to a more positive attitude towards their tube. The competition between the companies operating on different lines in the central area would undoubtedly encourage experimentation with new and better ranges of service and cheaper prices. Keeping train track and signals together would provide unified command which could be helpful in the confined spaces of tunnels and means there is no excuse for bad service as the operating company has all the necessary powers to sort out the problem.

In most cases stations serve just one line and would be in the same ownership as the track, signals and trains. In a limited number of cases there are interchange stations. At these locations each operating company would own the level of the station that it needed to maintain continuous ownership of the track for its line. The common parts allowing people to move from one line to another and reach the surface would be in the ownership of London Underground Limited. LUL would be charged with the duty of initiating common improvement projects at interchange stations and making sure that the property was exploited to provide the best possible service and property returns. Each individual company would be quite entitled to improve its section of the station adjacent to its tracks and would be entitled to carry out any platform and decorative improvements it chose to bring its part of the interchange station into line with its other stations.

Property Development Profits could be quite considerable. They would accrue to the individual tube companies earned from the ownership of single line stations and their adjacent property. In the case of the large interchange stations, they would be shared reflecting the proportionate inputs of property from the competing line companies and London Underground Limited.

The aim of this scheme would be to accelerate tube modernisation and improvement dramatically. Large sums of money would be raised. In this version we are talking about £6 billion of new equity and bond finance. The sums could be larger as it may be possible to raise £2.5 or £3 billion in new share issues and it may be possible to raise more than £4 billion, perhaps up to £6 billion in bond issues. We are therefore talking about a range of new finance from a minimum of £6 billion to a possible figure of £9 billion. This would enable accelerated improvements to be made. The new equity would be raised at the beginning and the bond money would be drawn down as and when the supplying industries could accommodate the demand for new trains, track improvement, signal improvement and new line tunnelling.

The House of Commons Select Committee on Transport, Local government and the Regions recently carried out a study of the London Underground. They concluded that the PPP deal was thoroughly undesirable. They stated "it is inevitable that the PPP will lead to significant and expensive disputes over the contracts and between staff and employers". They were very critical of the present government's policy even though the Committee has an in-built Labour majority. They drew attention to the continued under-financing of the railway and the substantial backlog in maintenance required. They were sceptical about how much risk had actually been transferred commenting that "under the PPP, the government has retained significant amounts of risk and will ultimately retain the responsibility for ensuring the continued running of the Underground". They recommended that the government ceased work on the PPP and tried to work out an alternative management plan in conjunction with Transport for London. They did not themselves evaluate TfL's proposal. They anticipate a shortfall in the amount of money available from the fare box and say that the government should move to meet such a shortfall. They support Crossrail and the Hackney / South West Line and make a number of important safety recommendations where they have considerable worries.

They also make a series of contingent recommendations on the assumption that despite their advice the government presses on with the PPP. They are extremely sceptical of the original idea that the PPP would save £4.5 billion compared with public sector management. In an unusually sharply worded conclusion, from a Labour dominated committee commenting on its own government, they state "a principal cause of the atrocious state of the London Underground has been the failure of the Treasury to provide adequate long-term funding over a number of decades. The Treasury is also, according to the evidence we received, one of the principal instigators of the PPP scheme. We were therefore appalled that despite its leading role it refused to make itself accountable to Parliament by giving evidence to the Sub-committee during the enquiry".

The most likely outcome of all this is continuing muddle and delay. No party seems to have enough control or political power to enforce its will and raise the necessary money to speed up modernisation of the Underground. During the later Conservative years substantial sums were invested in the Underground but most of this was pre-empted by the much delayed and very expensive Jubilee Line extension. This is an important new asset for London but it did use up a lot of the investment. Since that project has expired there has been a sharp reduction in the amount of public money going into the Underground at exactly the time when there should have been an acceleration in the expenditure used on upgrading and improving existing lines, especially the Piccadilly and Central Lines, where delays have become extremely worrying.

It would be possible to start again with an entirely new vision of a different kind of railway owned by Londoners and users of the system. Unfortunately, the future is likely to see continuing deterioration as more problems with existing assets come to light and as the rows over how to finance a solution intensify. It is unlikely the PPP will survive the full 30 years planned, and all too likely it will all need to be re-negotiated long before 2032. London Underground is over-stretched and under-financed. It carries a lot of strain for journeys into and out of the central area every working day. It is not such a serious alternative in the outlying parts of London where we desperately need new capacity and new routes as well. At the heart of our national transport and rail system lies the tube system. As all independent commentators and as Transport for London and the Parliamentary Select Committee know, it is in desperate need of new money and new management but there is no immediate relief in sight.

The third way for the tube would mean an expensive PPP where most of the risk remains with the taxpayer. The rows so far have delayed progress. As the government has its way, there will be disputes with the contractors, grappling with the complexity, and a continuing barrage of criticism from the Labour left. The third way means endless disappointment. The tube will continue to groan under the load placed upon it, as its managers wait for the investment they need. Many will regret the lack of competition and proper private sector involvement, for the PPP is unlikely to drive efficiency up to the necessary level.

Chapter seven

Britain's Roads – third way, no way

A shortage of motorways

THE UNITED KINGDOM IS a crowded island without access to a large motorway network. Competitor countries like France and Germany have many more good roads. Both France and Germany have more than three times as much motorway as the United Kingdom. France has slightly fewer people whilst Germany has a population of 81 million compared with the United Kingdom's 58 million. France is a little over twice the land area of the United Kingdom whilst Germany is about 40% bigger. The differences in land area and population would lead you to expect a closer comparison between the number of route miles of good highway in Britain, France and Germany.

The shortage of motorway space in Britain is just one symptom of the national dilemma. Private individuals prefer to spend ever-increasing sums of money on making sure they have their own car. Unfortunately for them, the provision of road space is largely a state owned monopoly that has failed to keep pace with the growing popularity of motoring as the main means of travel. Like all nationalised monopolies, the Highways Agency specialises in producing a poor service at a high price. It insists on creating artificial scarcity, relying on a kind of crude rationing resulting from increasing congestion. In this respect, it is just like the telephone system when it was a nationalised industry in the 1970's or like the tube system today. A potentially very popular activity is limited by the inadequacy of the supply.

In a very crowded island, where all of us wish to preserve what is best of the landscape, there is a physical limit on the amount of road space that can be created. Pressure groups against motorcars and road building have become extremely successful in the United Kingdom in recent years, putting off governments of all persuasions from road improvements. Germany put in much of her main highway network before the Second World War. France was able to press ahead in the second half of the twentieth century, with a much more centralised system of government overriding or ignoring any local voices of protest. In the United Kingdom, from the very early days of the motorway-building programme, opposition built up especially to urban motorways, which were so much more disruptive of existing property rights. The most recent improvements to the main motorway and trunk network, including the Newbury bypass and the M3 Winchester bypass, were hard fought battles with many protesters objecting strongly to tarmac over parts of the countryside.

As a result of a combination of a badly run government monopoly and the success of opposition groups to road schemes, Britain has emerged into the twenty-first century without a completed motorway network. The Romans built their roads. The eighteenth century built its canals, the nineteenth century its railways. Many of these routes were built on a tidal wave of public enthusiasm for progress or were built regardless of local antagonism at the time. In the twentieth century the planning system became a battleground for warring factions. Governments were prepared to ride roughshod over local opinion when it came to planning whole new settlements and communities, building new towns and massive extensions to existing smaller market towns, but became very worried about doing the same for the road network to service these communities.

Motorways are the safest roads by far in relation to the number of people using them. They are so much safer because pedestrians, cyclists and other vulnerable users are banned from them, just as they are banned from the railways. Traffic proceeding in different directions is separated, usually by a strong physical barrier. In addition, junctions are much safer. On single carriageway roads, most accidents occur at or near junctions. In the case of motorways, the junctions ensure the segregation of traffic moving in different directions, avoiding all head on or sideways collisions. When there is adequate capacity, motorways allow high average speeds of around 70 mph, offering a good, modern, fast, efficient means of travel. Britain has 3,465 kilometres of such road.

Trunk roads

Dual carriageway trunk roads can, at their best, come close to motorway levels of efficiency, speed and safety. The dual carriageway ensures reasonable segregation of traffic travelling in different directions. Now, in many cases, trunk roads also have grade-separated interchanges, reducing the risk of head on or sideways collision at junctions. In some cases, dual carriageways fall well short of motorway standards, with inadequate barriers between the two directions of traffic and with more dangerous light-controlled or roundabout junctions. Average speeds achieved on such roads are around 60 mph, almost 20% slower than that achieved on motorways, reflecting the more difficult junctions and people's greater caution, given the inferior road construction and speed limits. Great Britain has around 7,000 kilometres of such routes.

Other roads

The bulk of the main road network is still provided only to single carriageway standard whether trunk or principal A road. We have about 40,000 kilometres of such road. Outside urban areas most of this road has a maximum speed of 60 mph. Achieved average speeds of around 45 mph reflect congestion, dangerous bends and junctions and understandable caution on behalf of drivers. The table below shows the length of road in Great Britain divided up into the different standards of route. 58% of roads available are unclassified carrying relatively little of the traffic. A further 31% are B or C roads built to very modest standards. This leaves only a little over one tenth of the roads as principal roads, the bulk of which are still single carriageway. It is no wonder that Britain has so many traffic difficulties given the out of date and inadequate nature of the network compared with the number of cars and people trying to use it.

In recent years there has been a sharp decline in government interest in extending the road network of motorway and trunk roads. If we look at the number of lane kilometres started over the last ten years we can see there has been a precipitate decline from over 1,000 lane kilometres started in 1990/91 to only ninety-five started in 2000/01. In the last four years, under the Labour government, practically no new trunk road building has been started. There have been some completions, reflecting the delayed termination of works begun some years earlier.

In 1998, the new Labour government set out on a new policy. They reported in their document 'A New Deal for Trunk Roads in England': "On current projections and without policy changes traffic could grow by more than a third over the next twenty years and by more than a half on trunk roads. By 2016, a quarter of the trunk road network would be choked with traffic". They drew attention to research in 1994, which claimed that building new roads could generate extra traffic. This is a pretty unsurprising conclusion. In most other walks of life building new items is designed to satisfy and generate additional demand. The government sees nothing wrong with allowing house builders to build a large number of new houses even though the population of the country is not growing. They accept that people's needs and views of where they wish to live can change. No government minister would announce a ban on

Public road length: by class of road and country: 2000

					Kilometres
		England	Wales	Scotland	Great Britain
Motorways:					
	Trunk	2,900	137	384	3,421
	Principal	44	0	0	44
Dual Carriageway:					
	Trunk built-up	245	2	33	280
	Trunk non built-up	2,950	306	459	3,715
	Principal built-up	1,262	58	128	1,448
	Principal non built-up	1,292	115	90	1,497
Single Carriageway:					
	Trunk built-up	712	170	121	1,003
	Trunk non built-up	3,433	1,065	2,244	6,742
	Principal built-up	9,388	745	876	11,009
	Principal non built-up	12,866	1,676	6,326	20,868
B roads		19,784	2,969	7,304	30,057
C roads		63,108	9,834	10,329	83,271
Unclassified roads		181,831	15,861	30,657	228,349
Total		**299,815**	**32,938**	**58,951**	**391,704**

Source: Transport Statistics Great Britain 2001

New Construction 1990/91 - 2000/2001: motorway and trunk roads: England

		1990 /91	1991 /92	1992 /93	1993 /94	1994 /95	1995 /96	1996 /97	1997 /98	1998 /99	1999 /00	2000 /01
(a) Starts												
	Route km	263	196	117	213	79	6	159	0	10	20	10
	Lane km	1,024	836	467	947	282	50	839	0	65	126	95
(b) Completions												
	Route km	229	187	160	149	77	151	74	133	96	40	18
	Lane km	1,104	758	647	670	327	514	204	657	559	160	197

The figures in this table are outside the scope of National Statistics.

Source: Highways Agency

Please note that these tables are reproduced from original sources and we are therefore not responsible for any inaccuracies.

new house building on the grounds it might encourage more demand, yet more houses will use up more land and place more strain on the environment!

In 1998, in the same document, the government decided: "congestion will be treated as a transport problem open to a number of solutions – there will be no presumption in favour of new road building as an answer". They seriously hoped that there was a way of creating an integrated transport policy that would magic away the traffic growth. Four years later there has been absolutely no sign of the integrated transport policy arriving and every sign of the growing pressures on our road network as they correctly prophesied in their first paper on road building. The government set out to reduce the trunk road network and begun by transferring 40% of existing trunk roads to local authorities and downgrading them. They wished to keep only 60% of the inherited trunk road network, itself inadequate for the task of providing links between the main towns and cities in the country. In 1990, there were 500 road schemes outstanding. The Conservative government got cold feet about road building and scaled this down to 150 schemes by the time it left office in 1997. In some cases it was very sensible to cut roads out of the programme as they represented unacceptably damaging proposals. In other cases, it was recognition of the change of attitudes and a lack of money in the public sector to meet the commitments. The Labour government decided to hone 150 schemes down even further to thirty-seven that they thought could be started within the next seven years and withdrew a further thirty-six schemes completely from the programme.

By July 2000, and with the publication of the ten-year transport plan, the government's rhetoric had moved. They were coming under increasing pressure from the road lobby and users of motor vehicles to recognise that some increase in road capacity was necessary. They were beginning to appreciate that their famous integrated transport policy was not arriving or delivering in the way that they had hoped. In 1998 they had been able to claim they were diverting the money to road maintenance. By 2000, they proudly stated that the recent backlog of maintenance work had been eliminated. The government pointed out that less than 4% of the English road network (10,500 kilometres out of a total of 284,000 kilometres) is represented by trunk roads, yet those same roads carry 34% of all traffic and 67% of freight. The government recognised that 20% of the network is already heavily congested and much of the rest was also going to come under increasing pressure over the years ahead. Still not prepared to argue the need to build new roads, the government decided to smuggle in new road capacity by the back door in the hope that environmental groups would not notice. They decided on a policy of "adding capacity to the most congested corridors, largely by widening existing trunk roads". They proposed thirty trunk road bypasses, widening 5% of the strategic road network, eighty major schemes tackling bottle necks at other junctions and a series of smaller schemes elsewhere.

There was still no official recognition that roads are a necessary part of an integrated transport strategy. You need roads for buses to run on and for cars and taxis to take people to stations.

The Highways Agency

The Highways Agency is an executive agency of the Department of Transport, Local Government and the Regions. It is responsible for maintaining, operating and improving the strategic road network of motorways and trunk roads, which it currently values at £60 billion. It does this through eleven offices in nine different locations, with their headquarters in London. It employs 1,560 staff and is responsible for 4% of the total road length in the country.

The ten-year plan proposed £21 billion of investment in the strategic road network over ten years, an acceleration compared with the very low levels in the late 1990's. In 2002/2001 the Agency spent around half of its £1400 million on road maintenance.

The Agency has a series of improvements planned. It has forty-nine main schemes on the stocks at a cost of nearly £1.9 billion. In 2000/2001 the Agency completed the Manchester outer ring road, opening the final section of the M60 between Denton and Middleton. In east London it has awarded a contract for the privately financed A13 Thames Gateway project opening east/west access to Docklands, the lower Lee Valley and other Thames side locations. It is also examining the final completion of the A3 dual carriageway, offering a bypass for the village of Hindhead, whilst protecting the environment by putting through traffic in a 1.1mile twin-bored tunnel under Hindhead Common. The tunnel will take traffic away from the Devil's Punchbowl, a site of special scientific interest.

An overview of the motorway and trunk road network

Prior to the cull of schemes in 1990, the Department of Transport, Local Government and the Regions, proceeded with proposals for all the major trunk and principal roads in the country. The improvements were often carried out piecemeal, as if threading a string of beads. The combination of a lack of vision and worry about resistance led the Department to work up little schemes here and there, road by road, leaving Britain with a series of unfinished highways. There has been no recognition in the road construction programme of the big transfer of people, traffic and activity to the south east of the country. Nor has there been full recognition of the growing role of the east coast ports of Harwich and Felixstowe. The government did succeed in completing the London Orbital

Motorway, (M25), which did a great deal to improve transport links from all parts of the country to London, the south east and beyond to the continent. The road has been overwhelmed by its own success with regular congestion reflecting the large amount of traffic that does find it the quickest and best route to get from one part of the country to the other. The motorway and trunk road system was designed to be like the spokes of a wheel running out from the London hub.

The M2 takes traffic from London to Dover for access to the continent. The M2 itself only covers about half the distance and the A2 has still not been completely dualled in its southern section on the approach to Dover. The M2 is only a two-carriageway road in each direction and has been overwhelmed by the amount of traffic coming across the Channel. The M20 has been completed to Folkestone providing some necessary relief for cross-channel traffic. There is no dual carriageway route from London down to Hastings or Eastbourne. There is a good road to Brighton. Half its length is to motorway standard taking people to Gatwick Airport. The A24 from Leatherhead down to Bognor, Worthing and Brighton is still not fully dualled and the A3 to Chichester and Portsmouth from London still has the missing link at Hindhead. The M3 has been now completed to Southampton and there is a dual carriageway route on from Southampton to Bournemouth. The A31 has never been fully dualled beyond Ringwood to take people to Dorchester and the beauty spots of Dorset. The A303 should be the main highway to take people from the M3 down to Exeter. There are many gaps in the dual carriageway leading to frustration and delay, pollution and damage to villages all summer long as people try to use this principal holiday route. The A38 has not been fully dualled from Plymouth down to Cornwall and, whilst the A30 has been largely completed from Exeter to Cornwall, there are still one or two gaps causing holiday delays at the busy times of year.

The M4 is not large enough for the amount of traffic generated by the prosperous Thames Valley area and the need for good connections with London to the east and Bristol to the west. The M40 and the M1 provide reasonable links from London to the Midlands. The A1M has never been completed and there are still some difficult junctions on the A1 Great North Road from London to Leeds and beyond. The M11 only runs to Cambridge leaving an inadequate road across to Norwich. The A12 dual carriageway to Felixstowe is undersized for the current heavy weight of traffic wishing to get to the port. Traffic from the West Country to the

Midlands and the North, using the M5, finds a good road that is often heavily congested and in need of additional capacity. The A1/A1M ceases to be dualled north of Newcastle so there is no continuous dual carriageway to the east of the country up to Edinburgh. In Wales, the A465 Heads of the Valleys road, designed to link the dualled A40 to Swansea, has still not been completed although more capacity is needed for east/west travel to the valley towns. In North Wales, the A55 Expressway is a good road to take people from Merseyside to places like Conwy and Bangor but the road needs dualling all the way to Holyhead to service the Irish ferries. Across the country the A14 is a road under considerable pressure offering, as it does, access from the Midlands to Felixstowe. The capacity needs improving. Along the south coast the M27 is a relatively short motorway from just west of Southampton to Portsmouth. Parts of the A27 are now dual carriageway between Portsmouth and Eastbourne but there are also substantial gaps. Congestion is rife at peak hours of the day.

How should the network be improved?

This cursory examination of the inadequacies of the motorway and trunk network in England and Wales shows that a relatively modest increase in the mileage of trunk roads and motorways could make a considerable difference to the ability of the network to handle the traffic. Completion and widening of the M2/A2 to Dover would help with continental traffic. Completion of a dual carriageway from Eastbourne to Southampton would relieve a lot of the south coast pressures. Completion of a dual carriageway, the A303, all the way to Exeter and of the A30 all the way into Cornwall would provide better links to the West Country tourist destinations. More capacity on the M5, M4, and A14 and on sections of the M25 is much needed. Continuation of the A1 dual carriageway all the way to Edinburgh would provide a good alternative route for those seeking to go north of the border.

It is also important to use the available trunk and motorway space intelligently. The new Labour government began by thinking that it should segregate sections of carriageway on the trunk and motorway network for use by buses and taxis only. It began its experiment by placing a bus lane in the fast lane of the M4 eastbound into London. This particular proposal caused a furore as more and more people sat in cars in a long traffic jam whilst empty taxis and the occasional coach went by in an otherwise unused lane. The decision by the Prime Minister and his driver to use this lane when he wanted to get back to London in a hurry one day was not helpful to the cause of introducing such facilities on main motorways in the country. As a result of this particular battle, there has been a noticeable slowing down in government plans to reduce road space available to most vehicles on an already inadequate trunk and motorway network.

The Highways Agency is also experimenting with two other methods of trying to ration the available motorway space. The first system has been introduced on the M25. At busy times of the day overhead gantries contain warning lights imposing mandatory lower speed limits on traffic. The Agency claims that by imposing a 50 or 60 mile per hour maximum on traffic it can reduce the congestion. Casual observation suggests this is wrong. Delay is increased by frequent lane hopping rather than by traffic going at 70 mph instead of 60 mph when free to do so. Congestion is worst on the motorways where traffic is merging at junctions. If the Agency wishes to help reduce congestion at the peak it should turn its attention to designing longer merger lanes. The second experiment on the M27 is to adopt the American and Dutch idea of controlling flows onto the motorway by sensors and lights. At busy times where the motorway is close to its full capacity, traffic is held at light controlled junction entrances to solve the problems of merging traffic.

The environmental arguments

Environmentalists are right to say that road building can be very disruptive to the landscape. No sensible person wishes to see more and more of our green fields swallowed up under concrete or tarmac, whether it be for new housing estates or for new roads. In recent years, however, environmentalists should appreciate that most of the spoiling of the landscape has taken place through the construction of new housing estates and industrial parks, which in their turn, place more pressures on an already inadequate road network in the areas of densest new construction. The most intrusive environmental transport project in recent years has been the cross-channel rail link that has carved its way through the Kent countryside, doing as much damage as a large road would have done. What we need to do is to have a plan for how much of our green and pleasant landscape we can lose to all building purposes over any given time period. We should give roads their fair ration within this total, gearing the construction of the roads to the construction of the new homes, factories, shops and other facilities that the plans permit.

Of course it is also important to try to be sensitive when any new road is being constructed. There are two examples in the current programme where tunnels are being considered for very good environmental reasons. It would be good to complete the A3 dual carriageway and even better if that can be done in a way that reduces traffic stress on the Devil's Punchbowl, an area of outstanding natural beauty. Similarly, it would be good if the dual carriageway A303 could be completed to the West Country whilst, at the same time, improving the environment around Stonehenge, a World Heritage Centre site. Current proposals include tunnelling through the Stonehenge area to take the traffic out of the landscape.

Sometimes construction of a new road produces environmental gains as well as environmental losses. In the case of the construction of a dual carriageway A303, this has to be balanced against the loss of fields that the new road will impose and the big improvement in the environment in the villages which are currently cut in half by the thundering traffic on the main roads going through them. A good case can be made out for many a bypass on the 'balance of advantages' argument.

The government will face a battle over some of its road widening schemes. It was hoping that by shifting from so-called new highway construction to road widening and saying a great deal about the need to do it in an environmentally sensitive way, they would avoid battles with environmental groups. However, there are already protesters extremely worried about the widening of the M42 near Birmingham, and about plans to widen the M66 across the Pennines through the Eden Valley. In each case the government will have to examine whether there are better ways of protecting the local environment or whether there are some other changes that can be made elsewhere to provide better environmental gains.

When I was responsible for the Welsh road programme I was keen to dual the A465 Heads of the Valleys road and found there was a great deal of support from towns like Merthyr Tydfil for such a proposal. They saw that a good dual carriageway road from Swansea to England, going close to the town centres, would be extremely helpful for jobs and prosperity. At the same time I cancelled all the schemes proposed for the A5, especially on the old Telford road through Snowdonia. The scenery was breathtakingly beautiful and the road full of so much history. It seemed a great pity to propose a clumsy modern widening scheme over such a beautiful landscape. It seemed to me a much better idea to route main lorry traffic along the A55 Northern Expressway, a road largely completed, rather than trying to wrestle with the A5 and turning it into a highway suitable for juggernauts. Similarly in the south of England, if we decided to complete the dualling of the A24, which is almost complete, there would be no need for such projects on the A22, and if we complete the A303 we will reduce some of the pressure on the M5.

Cutting pollution and jams requires a good system of trunk routes allowing free flowing traffic as often as possible. Progress being made through technology with cutting pollution needs reinforcing with a bigger and better trunk and motorway network.

Local roads

An extensive system of local roads in Britain has developed over the centuries. Progress has been made from cart tracks and private farm routes to a complicated network of tarmacadam public highways. In the twentieth century, new settlements were built with an eye to vehicle travel. Each new close, avenue, road and street is carefully connected to the local highway network and usually the local council, who take over responsibility for their maintenance, supervision and safety, adopts the roads. Whilst the roads remain under the control of local councils it is a truly national network with similar signs, standards of construction and safety rules, county by county and district by district. Local roads are multi-purpose highways used by all types of vehicle. They are used for short and long journeys, for shopping, leisure, work, journeys to school and deliveries. It has been a most successful network because it is very flexible and because you can get by motor vehicle to practically every address in the country.

In recent years there has been a national move towards restricting vehicle speeds and use of the comprehensive local highway network. Councils and people are naturally worried about death and injury on the roads. Because the local roads are multi-purpose, there are dangers in the conflict between vulnerable traffic like bicycles and pedestrians, versus better-protected vehicles, like lorries, vans and cars. The local road network is interspersed with thousands of junctions and often comprises narrow, winding, hilly, routes where visibility can be poor. Vehicles travelling in different directions have to use the same bit of highway and people often decide to pause or park along stretches of the local road network.

Councils are right to take action to tackle accident blackspots and try to improve the safety design of the highway. They are also right to take action to restrict parking and unloading where highways are narrow and where indiscriminate parking or unloading serves to impede or prevent the flow of other vehicles wishing to use the road. Councils are right to consider how pedestrians could be better served if they had proper pavements to walk on and decent crossing points when they need to get across a road.

However, these legitimate concerns have spilled over into a very wide range of traffic management measures that do not always help safety but usually impede traffic flow on the local highway network. Many different approaches have been adopted to try to reduce speeds of vehicles on local roads, especially in urban areas. Two different types of speed camera have been introduced. The traditional sort entails placing a camera in a big box to take a photograph of any vehicle above the target speed. These cameras have been successful in reducing speeds where they are located, although at times they cause braking and bunching as vehicles approach the measured area. Digital cameras are now being introduced which measure the time taken by a vehicle over a specified stretch of highway. From the authority's point of view they are superior, as they do not require replacement film.

A number of other devices are being introduced to slow speeds in urban areas that go much further than prosecuting people who break the rules. On many roads, sleeping policemen or traffic humps have been introduced. These do considerable damage to a car's suspension and provide an extremely uncomfortable ride, especially for anyone who is disabled or injured. Drivers of the emergency vehicles, police, ambulances and fire engines, also find these extremely difficult, slowing down their access to an emergency. A variant of the road hump, the cushion, can encourage the very kind of dangerous driving the traffic management systems are designed to reduce or stop. The placing of traffic cushions on either side of the road, partial humps, leads some drivers to try and drive up the middle of the road straddling the two directions of the carriageway to try and avoid the humps altogether. Larger vehicles can continue at a speed they choose because the cushions do not affect them, as they are wider than the obstacles.

The most extraordinary idea of all to slow vehicles down has been to remove one of the two carriageways of a road completely by placing kerbs and bollards in strategic locations and putting up signs giving priority to one direction or the other. Drivers then have to make fine judgments about whether they can proceed safely on the remaining piece of carriageway before a car coming in the other direction reaches the same spot of road. This design of highway increases the number of occasions that drivers will make a misjudgement leading to an accident.

In many places aggressive high kerbs have been introduced to slow people on bends and at junctions and parts of the carriageway have often been removed to narrow the road at junctions to change driver behaviour. Many more pedestrian crossings and light controlled systems for giving pedestrians priority have been introduced, especially in London.

The Transport Road Research Laboratory investigated the impact of nine different traffic-calming measures upon pollution and vehicle speeds. They examined 75mm high flat top road humps running across the whole road, 80mm high round top humps, 1.7m wide speed cushions, the combination of a pinch-point in the road and a speed cushion, a raised junction where the whole surface of the junction had been elevated, a chicane, a build-out where the road had been narrowed deliberately, a mini roundabout, and 1.9m wide cushions. The experiment showed that speed reduction was greatest with flat top humps and least with speed cushions. The 100mm high raised junction achieved a 12 mph reduction in average speed, the 75mm flat top hump and the 80mm round top hump, a 10 mph reduction in speed, the mini roundabout an 8 mph reduction in speed, and the pinch-point with a speed cushion a 7 mph reduction in speed.

All the traffic calming measures also had a substantial impact upon the amount of pollution generated by vehicles travelling in the effected area. The study concluded: "for petrol non-catalyst, petrol catalyst, and diesel cars, the increases in the mean emissions of CO were 34%, 59%, and 39% respectively. For each vehicle category the increase in mean HC emissions was close to 50% ... NOx emissions from diesel vehicles increased by about 30%. Emissions of CO_2 increased by 20 to 26%, with the increase being significant for each type of vehicle. For diesel vehicles, emissions of particulate matter increased by 30%".

However, had the study concentrated on cars with catalysts which are being introduced rapidly across the vehicle fleet, the increases would have been much bigger. In another study by Zhger and Blessing in 1995 it was found that CO and NOx emissions from a single catalyst equipped petrol car increased by 160% and 900% respectively after the introduction of road humps. It was also found that outputs from catalyst cars are very variable. Cars with catalytic systems normally have low emissions when travelling in a straight line without too much acceleration but the emissions shoot up with frequent stopping and starting and acceleration. Drivers tend to accelerate quite swiftly between humps and obstacles as they are trying to compensate for their perceived loss of time in surmounting these obstacles. This is bad news for pollution. (See Appendix 1)

The combined effect of all of this has been to make many motorists feel that they are the villains whose interests are always ignored. There does not seem to be any balance. Wherever there is a worry about conflict between different types of road users it appears that the motorist has to be regulated into discomfort.

Traffic managers should think again and should think a bit more clearly about how safety can be improved whilst traffic is allowed to flow freely. They should first of all make a distinction between their treatment of main A and B roads and the small, often residential roads, connected to them. It is quite right to have relatively low speed limits in residential areas, near schools, hospitals and other institutions. Cameras can best enforce these speed limits, leaving the carriageway as clear as possible to make it easier to make progress and avoid conflicts between vehicles. Wherever possible these roads should have good pavements to keep pedestrians segregated from traffic and able to walk safely with clearly identified crossing points at regular intervals. These crossing points are best at light controlled junctions placed in clearly visible locations. Pedestrians should be discouraged from walking in the road, just as vehicles should be banned from driving on the pavements. It should be an offence to park, whether for unloading or for some other purpose, in a position which blocks a carriageway or entranceway.

The main A and B roads should be treated rather differently. The intention should be to improve junction design thereby encouraging the free flow of traffic. On busy A roads, footbridges or underpasses should be provided to allow speedy crossing of the road at no risk to the individual. Junctions should be widened rather than narrowed and, wherever possible, left and right hand turning traffic segregated from traffic going straight on. Cars should be allowed to turn left on a red light, treating the red light the same as a stop sign. Wherever possible villages and small urban settlements should be bypassed by A roads, reducing the potential for conflict between pedestrians and vehicles. Sight lines and visibility need to be improved wherever possible. Sometimes this can be done by elongating and widening the kerb. In other places, where room does not permit, more mirrors should be introduced so that drivers can see the bend.

Parking is an important part of the equation. If parking is too restricted or too expensive, it can lead to a large number of vehicles searching for spaces in congested urban areas and adding to the general traffic problem. Too much on-street parking interrupts the flow of traffic and restricts the amount of road space available. It interrupts the flow still further as people try and reverse into small parking spaces. The absence of good parking is often one of the main reasons why people will not leave their car at the station and take a train or tube. Very few bus stations and bus stops have car parks adjacent to allow car to bus transfer. It makes injury to pedestrians more likely, as they emerge from behind parked cars to cross the road.

Meanwhile the planners in the new suburban areas are busily accommodating the cars that people wish to buy and own. The two-garage home is now quite normal and some larger houses are now provided with three garages and additional hard-standing parking space. Each district needs to review its car parking strategy, trying to substitute off-street car parking for on-street car parking places, trying to make sure there are enough car parking places adjacent to main transport interchanges with train and bus services and ensuring that when new shops and offices are constructed, the transport issues have all been thought through and sufficient provision made. The present fashion to restrict the number of parking places in town without improving train and bus services sufficiently to compensate is merely adding to the stress on an already overburdened road system.

The future of the car

It seems very likely that people are going to want more and more flexible transport of their own. Young people tend to have a great deal of sympathy for the green cause. They do not wish to see the planet destroyed by pollution. However, they also strongly express the wish to take their driving test as soon as possible and to get access to a car of their own at the first available opportunity. When I was a student it was a very rare undergraduate who had a car. Most of us were happy to live life without one accepting that a car was something you aspired to when you had a job and an income. Today's generation of students regards a car as a necessity with many of them managing to own or use one on a regular basis. Schools with sixth forms have to make provision for senior pupils to come to school by car. Universities have to tarmac over large areas on the campus to provide parking places and many parents are put under pressure to make a financial contribution to make it all possible. The new generation is saying very clearly that it wants to have access to its own personal, flexible transport.

Most motorists will be delighted if technical progress enables us to get rid of all or most of the pollution generated by motor vehicles. They will also be delighted if road design and vehicle design can make further strides forward in reducing the likelihood of accidents that endanger life or limb. What is unlikely, is that a new generation will emerge who are prepared to sacrifice the idea of personal, flexible transport altogether. People have got too used to the idea that they do not have to brave the wind and rain from their door to the bus stop or the train station. They like the convenience of a car or van at their home to take them where they wish, when they wish, with whatever luggage they require.

To accommodate this we need to tame the car and improve the streets. We need to make the public transport alternative so much better so that on busy routes, at busy times of the day, many more people will easily and naturally switch from their car to the train or the bus. We also need to ensure that our road improvement and parking policies are compatible with people's day-to-day travel needs. There is currently an over supply of motor vehicles in the new car market. Competition law is gradually putting pressure on the motor manufacturers to release their surplus cars at cheaper prices. The British system of franchised dealers having a monopoly over the provision of their own particular brand of car to the market is being broken up by the intervention of anti-cartel European legislation. Manufacturers are alert to the opportunities of producing cheap, attractive, reliable vehicles to sell into the mass market. Cheap lease, hire purchase and loan finance is making it so much easier for people to buy the good value vehicles currently on offer. We must assume that a rising proportion of the population will own a car. As more and more women go out to work so they learn to drive or purchase a vehicle. Each succeeding generation is more car bound than the preceding one and most now are brought up to believe that a car will be a natural part of their adult lives. The country will continue to spend more on new car purchases than on investment in public transport. We need to redress the balance, freeing the private markets to put a bigger commitment behind the bus and train so that it has some chance of providing an attractive rival, in the places and at the times when it can have the most beneficial effect.

Third Way finance has had little impact on road travel. Most of it is already in the private competitive market. The government's main aim has been to use tax and regulation to limit the popularity and success of the private market in offering flexible travel. The government is attracted to raising private money for toll roads and is building the first in Birmingham. The government's adviser on transport, Sir John Birt, has recommended more such roads. Time will tell if the government wants to take the environmentalists on to bring this about.

Chapter eight

Waterways – a story of public sector decline

Early history

BEFORE THE REIGN OF Elizabeth I a limited number of rivers were navigable in Britain. There was fierce competition to use the waterways. Mill owners wished to harness the energy of the stream. Fishermen wished to use fish weirs to make their trade easier. Navigable stretches of the Thames, the Lea, the Yorkshire Ouse, the Kentish Star and other rivers were under the care of corporations who had legislative force to clean up the rivers and keep navigation open. Corporations like London, Gloucester and York had powers to interfere with private property in order to allow the passage of boats. Under an Act of Henry VIII, Commissions of Sewers were established to deal with drainage and flood prevention. They could levy a rate upon the landowners affected.

From the reign of Elizabeth onwards there was a keen interest in restoring navigation on rivers where it was all but impossible. Letters of Patent were often granted to individuals to take on this task or powers were granted to a company. These individuals were often given power to collect tolls from all those who used the improved navigation. In some cases they were granted monopoly rights to carry goods on the river. The prospectors dredged rivers, removed obstructions, banged the heads of the fishermen and the mill owners, and from Elizabeth's reign onwards introduced the pound lock. In the seventeenth century efforts were intensified. Between 1662 and 1665, following the Civil War, 685 miles of river navigation was possible. There were attempts to drain the Fens but Parliament insisted on keeping the rivers navigable. Acts of Parliament were passed to deal with the Worcestershire Stour, the Wye, the Lugg, the Medway, the Hampshire Avon and the Itchen.

There was a second period of vigorous activity from 1697 to 1700. Acts of Parliament were passed for the navigation of the Tone, the Aire, the Calder, the Trent, the Lark, and the Bristol Avon. A third period of hyperactivity from 1719 to 1721 saw a number of Acts passed to improve navigation at the time of the South Sea Bubble. Acts were passed for the Derbyshire Derwent, the Douglas, the Idle, the Kennet, the Weaver, the Mersey, and the Irwell. The 685 miles of navigable river in 1660 increased to 1160 miles by 1724. Increasing volumes of goods were moving in coastal shipping and up the rivers. For example, York received coal from Newcastle by ship to the Humber and then in smaller vessels up the Ouse. London also received its coal by sea from Newcastle.

The coming of canals

Canals began to blossom from the middle of the eighteenth century. The St Helens Canal was authorised by Act of Parliament in 1755, to link the Mersey near Sankey Bridges to St Helens. In 1759, an Act was passed for a canal from Worsley to Salford and from Worsley to Hollin Ferry on the Mersey below the Irwell Junction, to carry coal in the Manchester area. The canal was finished in 1761 and was widely praised for its engineering sophistication. In places it went underground and in one place it went over a navigable river.

The large number of canals built were all financed by limited liability companies drawing on private capital. Those with coal and minerals to sell took stakes, keen to promote cheaper transport for their product. Local professional people, landowners and tradesmen were enthusiastic buyers of shares, seeing the opportunity for profit. Money was raised in the early stages to plan the project and to lobby Parliament for the necessary legislation. More money was then raised by subscription, once the Parliamentary Act was through, to carry out the necessary engineering works. Very often there was strong opposition from local landowners and from local tradesmen who feared the impact the canal might have upon the drainage of their land or upon the markets for their produce.

A number of engineers including Bindley, Telford, Rennie and Outram developed considerable expertise in deciding the route and designing the structures needed to carry the canal.

The canal heyday

As the network neared completion in the 1820's and 1830's, some of the early investment proved to be extremely worthwhile. In 1833, the seven leading companies were all showing handsome profits to founding shareholders.

At the other end of the spectrum companies like Grand Western, Bude, Salisbury and Southampton, and the Leominster never paid dividends. The later the canal was constructed, the dearer the cost and the less likely shareholders to get an acceptable return.

Decline

Once the railway era started in earnest, canals were doomed to decline. The railways began by succeeding primarily with passengers but as the Victorian period wore on the railways picked up more and more freight. The railway industry was keen to take over the waterway competition. Parliament in 1873 and finally in 1888 blocked such an avenue of expansion. The canals tried to compete by cutting prices to keep bulk goods traffic. They sometimes succeeded in maintaining the volume of use, but suffered sharp declines in revenues, profits and dividends and lost out in the general increase in trade as the Victorian prosperity machine got into gear.

Nationalisation

In the twentieth century, decline continued. The canals were taken over during the Second World War and were finally nationalised in 1948. The Manchester Ship Canal, completed at the end of the nineteenth century, was left out of the nationalisation as it was regarded as part of the Manchester Docks. The Thames Conservancy was also omitted. The nationalised industry did not discover the secret of turning the canals back into a serious means of travel for large quantities of freight. Indeed, in the early days of nationalised control, the network continued to lapse into a poor state of maintenance and repair. Over the years a number of canals silted up, some of them were tarmacked over to make way for new roads and many of the big engineering structures have decayed.

Current state of the canals

Reporting on the year to 31 March 2001, the British Waterways Board claimed that a safety related maintenance backlog amounted to £56.9 million. Only 60% of the canal network had been dredged to a satisfactory standard and numerous lock gates needed replacing, tunnels and bridges needed repairing and canals needed linking again

The canal network in Britain is a hidden asset. Currently in receipt of a £62 million grant from the Department for Transport, Local Government and the Regions, British Waterways Board, until recently, has been very slow to build up its trading income despite the obvious opportunities open to it. The canal company can sell water where it is needed, transporting the water around the canal system on behalf of water companies. Last year, water sales did increase by 51%, but are still only running at £1.7 million per year. The company has important wayleaves to run utility cables and pipes. The recent telecommunications joint venture Ipsaris (formerly Fibreway) was the main contributor in the year to March 2001 to growing income from business. Very little goods traffic now runs on the canals, a missed marketing opportunity.

Leisure income increased last year by 16% to £17.4 million. Principal sources were craft licences and mooring income raised from owners and hirers of narrow boats. The biggest potential of the canal system lies in property development. Canalside property is potentially very valuable. Particularly in urban areas the canalside location provides an ideal backdrop for commercial and residential development. Last year, property income reached a new high of £26.4 million including the rentals from investment properties that BWB have helped develop over the years.

In the dying days of the nineteenth century, the canals showed that they could still play a useful role in British transport needs. They did so by offering low cost, relatively slow, bulk freight handling. The network was made more attractive by linking it, as with the Manchester Ship Canal, to major ports where goods could be trans-shipped into larger vessels. Under nationalisation, in the second half of the twentieth century, the canals were allowed to decline dramatically. Attention shifted to motor transport and the ubiquitous lorry took over from both the canal barge and the railway freight wagon.

How can the canals fight back?

The present board of management of British Waterways is trying to restore the canals. They are attracting substantial sums of grant, charitable money, millennium funding and the like into the task of restoring the canals. They are dredging, improving structures and sometimes adding new links. They are particularly proud of the Falkirk Wheel, an important modern boatlift linking two navigable waterways. They are finding it is quite possible to attract enthusiasts and volunteers to help with the work and to help raise the money. The boating community, using the canals for leisure purposes, is proving a strong ally in carrying out this important rehabilitation.

The board has been less adept at defining a proper commercial future for the business. It would undoubtedly be better if British Waterways Board were converted into a public limited company and new capital raised by selling shares on the stock market. To do this, the business would need to develop several elements in its current mixture of revenues to show that it had a potentially viable and profitable future.

The government would probably be prepared to give it some

kind of cash limited grant for a specified number of years. This could be less than the government would otherwise spend on owning the operation but sufficient to allow British Waterways Board to continue with its programme of capital works improvement. The grant should be released against specified projects designed to increase the navigable sections of the network. The prime aim should be to increase revenue from the three most obvious sources.

The first and the easiest area to rapidly drive forward is property development. There are many sites adjacent to the leading canals in the system ripe for substantial development. As British Waterways Board has shown on a modest scale so far, it is possible to find joint venture partners and for British Waterways Board to retain an interest in the property once it has been redeveloped. The company could build up an impressive rent roll from its property activities as well as, from time to time, selling investment properties as it does at the moment to release cash. The waterfront at Nottingham is one example of what can be achieved when successful schemes are put in place.

The second thrust of business development should be in developing the commercial use, which can be made of the wayleaves and the water. The canals represent a water grid in Britain. More water could be routed from rainy and wet parts of the country to the large users of water who are looking for more competitive prices than those offered by their local monopoly suppliers. A number of people are trying to put together deals along these lines but are encountering some delay on the part of British Waterways Board. This could become an extremely important business for BWB. Similarly, BWB has now made rather better strides in developing the wayleaves business with the telecommunications industry but there is far more scope for cables and pipes of all kinds to take advantage of the flat straight routes offered by the canal system in many parts of the country. It can provide a relatively cheap and easy answer to those wishing to put in more pipe and cable network capacity and a relatively easy source of income for BWB.

Thirdly, we need to use the waterways themselves. When visiting canals or seeing video of the improvements carried out by BWB the observer is struck by the very low level of use, particularly by working boats. On a good summer weekend the leisure uses of the canal can be high, but throughout the working week in winter, very little moves on the canal system. As revenues from tolls and mooring charges will be incremental and marginal, it should be quite possible for British Waterways to stimulate interest by relatively low levels of charge to get freight moving again on the canal system. It also requires good interchange facilities at specified points along the canal to local distribution systems by lorry or van and onto ships for coastal or overseas routing at the leading ports. The canals and navigable rivers are Britain's forgotten highways, with considerable scope for taking some of the burden off the roads. Sensible pricing is the way to trigger this improvement.

The task of privatising BWB would be a relatively straightforward and easy one. The Board should be converted to a plc and proposals drawn up for the sale of new shares. At the same time, the government could cut its existing shareholding if it so wished. Given the monopoly position the company would enjoy on most of the major water transport routes and, given the scope for property development profits, it should be possible to forecast reasonable profitability for the new company. There would be no need for monopoly type controls on the freight, property or wayleaves businesses, as they are competing fully against clear choices. There might need to be some cap upon charges to private narrow boat owners and leisure users, as owners of such boats are captive customers of the waterways company.

Third Way finance for British Waterways means complex partnerships, usually between different recipients of government grants. They use the language of PPP but in practice, outside commercial property development on the canal bank, there is so far very little private sector interest in carrying the risk.

The table shows that Britain still conducts a substantial trade through her coastal ports. It also shows that London has now lost her pre-eminence, eclipsed by the volumes at Grimsby and Immingham and at Tees and Hartlepool. Milford Haven is large because it is a main port for handling oil and Sullom Voe is large because all its volume is accounted for by bulk fuel. London is still the largest port for mixed cargoes, other than bulk fuel, reflecting the diversity of activity in the capital city. Grimsby and Immingham, Tees and Hartlepool, London, Forth and Sullom Voe between them account for 40% of all the weight of goods handled. Ten other ports handled in excess of 10 million tons in 2000, accounting for a further 38% of all UK traffic. Grimsby and Immingham has a substantial coal trade, Port Talbot a substantial oil trade and Newport, iron and steel products. When it comes to passenger movements, Dover is the dominant port. In 2000, 16.198 million people moved through the

Shipping and ports

Freight moved through ports - 2000	Thousands of Tons
All East Coast Scotland	112,889
All Thames and Kent	82,970
All Humber	77,711
All North East	56,422
Grimsby and Immingham	52,501
Tees and Hartlepool	51,473
London	47,892
All Lancs and Cumbria	45,004
All Sussex and Hants	42,653
Forth	41,143
All West and North Wales	38,719
Sullum Voe	38,204
All Southern East Anglia	36,751
Southampton	34,773
Milford Haven	33,768
Liverpool	30,421
All Bristol Channel	29,699
Felixstowe	29,686
Orkneys	22,798
All Northern Ireland	21,434
All Scotland, West Coast	17,623
Dover	17,434
Medway	15,292
Belfast	12,484
Port Talbot	11,725
Hull	10,722
Bristol	9,647
Manchester	7,687
Clyde	7,224
All West Country	6,722
All Wash and Northern East Anglia	4,452
All United Kingdom Port Traffic	573,050

Souce: DTLR Transport Statistic report ñ Maritime Statistics 2000 TSO 2001

Please note that these tables are reproduced from original sources and we are therefore not responsible for any inaccuracies.

Port of Dover compared with 28.9 million passenger movements through all other ports. The next largest to Dover was Portsmouth with 3.176 million passenger movements.

A great deal of freight now moves by roll-on roll-off ferry with powered vehicles accompanying trailers. In the UK, 544,000 of these vehicles were plying their trade in the year 2000 compared with 990,000 coming to the UK from the rest of the European Union. There has been a particularly rapid build up in France from 131,000 in 1990 to 339,000 in 2000 and in the Benelux countries from 37,000 in 1990 to 114,000 in the year 2000.

Britain's pre-eminence as a shipping nation was based on very successful coastal trades with water borne transport extending up the rivers and onto canal barges to penetrate to most of the industrial and urban centres of the country. The decline and decay of the inland waterways has been complemented by a reduction in the amount of coastal trade being conducted. Shipping has maintained its edge for bulk cargoes like crude oil, petroleum products, liquid chemicals and ores. It has found it increasingly difficult to compete for the multitude of commodities, products and finished goods that characterise the complex trade of an advanced, industrial country. Dover has risen to success based on its capacity to handle a procession of heavy lorries taking goods to and from the continent and on its ability to provide a good service to a large number of passengers. Felixstowe has developed similar strengths, placing ever more strain upon the A14 road that has to take the articulated lorries. The Port of London has gravitated downstream as the size of ships has increased, making access through the relatively narrow and shallow waters of the Thames more difficult. The great western ports of Bristol and Liverpool had their heyday in the eighteenth and early nineteenth centuries with the triangular trade and another flourish in the Second World War when so much supply came across the Atlantic. They have faced a relative decline as the pattern of our bulk trades has shifted eastwards favouring the east coast ports and the links with the continent.

Links to ports

Successive governments have not been good at encouraging strong road links to our ports. Dover still does not have continuous motorway to link it to London and the rest of the country. It is also now under competitive attack from the Folkestone/Cheriton rail freight link across the Channel. Whilst this has proved disappointing, operating currently at only about a third of its planned levels, it does nonetheless take an important part of Dover's trade away. The intention is that freight traffic should build up rapidly through the Channel link as the rail links around London are improved to provide more capacity and faster journey times. Recent progress with rail freight across the Channel has been badly dented by difficulties in policing the Sangatte Terminal on the French side of the link. The decision of the French authorities to locate a refugee centre here has made it extremely difficult for freight operators. Night after night they find that asylum seekers and economic migrants are keen to jump over the wire fence and attach themselves in dangerous positions to trains in the hope of hitching a lift to Britain. This has led to more and more security and to the partial closure of the freight facilities from time to time.

There has been a similar decline in the weight of tonnage registered in the United Kingdom and sailing the world, plying its trade. At the beginning of 2001 the world had a merchant fleet of 332.2 million dead weight tons. Only 7.1 million tons or 2% of this was registered in the United Kingdom. Panama with 58.9 million tons, Liberia with 43.4 million tons, Greece with 26.1 million tons, Malta with 21.8 million tons and Norway with 21.2 million tons dominated the lists. The presence of relatively small places like Liberia and Panama at the top of the lists of tonnages registered in the world showed that it is nothing to do with the trading potential and the goods generated by a country. Britain built a very big merchant marine on the back of very successful bulk trades of its own, creating a trade in wool, textiles, coal, steel and manufactured goods. In recent decades the United Kingdom has lost her once dominant position in merchant shipping as ship owners have found other jurisdictions like Liberia and Panama much more sympathetic to their needs. These jurisdictions have made a concerted effort to encourage ship ownership and registration. They have kept their taxes low, their regulatory requirements light and have shown themselves very friendly to the ship owning business. Britain like many of the other advanced, heavily regulated and quite highly taxed countries has seen her relative and absolute position decline as a result of these changes.

UK government policy towards shipping

It is surprising how hostile United Kingdom governments have been to maritime and shipping endeavour given the very strong historical success in these areas and the natural advantages of Britain's location and geography to ship-borne trade.

The present government claims to wish to revitalise shipping ports in the United Kingdom. Their policy sets out "to maximise the vital economic contribution that shipping and ports make to our prosperity". They have made some limited tax changes that have been helpful to ship owners. They then go on immediately to set out as their prime objectives the need to minimise pollution and improve safety. In December 1998, they published 'British Shipping: Charting a New Course' that contained thirty action points. One of the main recommendations was to introduce a tonnage tax regime that took place in the Finance Act 2000.

Their policy paper 'Modern Ports: a UK Policy' issued in

November 2000, was also full of warm words about the need to have a comprehensive policy on ports to create "successful safe and sustainable ports that are fully integrated into the transport system". To do this the government states its aims are to: (i) support the role of UK ports in maintaining UK and regional competitiveness (ii) develop and encourage the use of nationally agreed high safety standards in docks and harbour waters (iii) promote the best environmental practice for port development and port operations (iv) build on the integrated approach detailed in Transport 2010 which recognised the importance of port hubs. Amidst so many fine words about training, safety improvement and sustainable development there is no action plan designed to tackle the most obvious difficulties facing ports and merchant shipping in Britain. There is no intention to bring the costs of owning and running ships in Britain more in line with those in Panama, Liberia and the other successful ship owning places. This would require bold moves on the tax front, which the government seems unwilling to take. Secondly, there are no plans to tackle the main bottlenecks of getting to the ports by road and rail for trans-shipment by boat. Many of Britain's ports are now very remote from the prime road network, the main commercial arteries of the country. The east and south coast ports are out on something of a limb with inadequate links to the rest of the country. Rail freight has been suffering from poor management and a lack of ambition until privatisation. It began to recover only to be badly damaged by the general problems facing the railways that we have detailed above.

If the government is truly serious about expanding British ports and having more goods and passengers moving by sea it needs to take urgent and immediate action to link the principal ports to the main road and rail networks much more firmly and provide the extra capacity that they require.

A better vision for shipping in Britain

A visionary government, concerned about our environment and wishing to tackle the problems of inadequate capacity on all our transport networks, would take seriously the possibility of integrating inland barge traffic with coastal shipping, cross-channel shipping and trans-Atlantic shipping from our main ports. The canal network can give us access to a large number of urban and industrial locations. It could provide a cheap and relatively easy way of transporting goods where they are not time sensitive. The ports should be able to collect goods from lorries, freight trains and inland barges to ship in bulk quantities to markets on the continent and further afield. It should also be possible to resume more coastal traffic around the United Kingdom given that many of the large centres of population like London, Liverpool and Manchester, Teeside and Tyneside are on or close to the coast. It will require more development of jetties and wharves, the provision of cranes and trans-shipment points and the development of more interchangeable containers between lorries, barges, freight wagons and ships. The canals should not just be a romantic trip into the past for the dedicated minority that own narrow boats or wish to hire them. They should also be a trip into the future for those with bulk goods to move at an economic price. The canals can also provide suitable conduits for more pipes and wires to provide pipeline and cable networks to carry fluids and the main modern commercial traffic, information and messages.

The government should set itself the objective of rebuilding Britain as a truly maritime nation. Give British ship owners and ship traders a more favourable tax regime and there could be rapid growth. Create the right physical links to the ports and they could become a preferred route for more traffic. Work at a more commercial approach from the canal and navigable river system and that could start to take some of the strain off the roads and railway lines. Soon hundreds of harbours, berths, quays and jetties would bloom around the inland and coastal waterways. Soon we would begin to see a true pattern of commercial use developing for Britain's hidden network.

London's river

If you wish to see an unused transport asset there is no better place for this than the Thames through London. The Thames is a super-highway dividing the City between north and south. In the sixteenth and seventeenth centuries it was the central highway of the City. Wharves, piers and jetties sprouted along the riverbanks on both sides with many people offering freight and passenger services along the river. It was usually the quickest and safest way to travel from east to west or west to east within a congested city.

The Mayor's transport strategy issued in July 2001, genuflected towards the importance of the river. The document points out that around 3 million people a year travel on the Thames by boat and many more walk the Thames-side footpaths. What these figures do not reveal is that many of these are tourists using the Thames as a source of pleasure cruises to see the sights from the river. There is little serious use of the river for London commuters even though it potentially offers very good routes from Westminster to the City, from the City to Docklands or from Docklands to Chelsea or Hammersmith. (See Appendix 2)

Under the Mayor's strategy they are examining further piers, looking at extending the passenger services, improving their regularity and frequency and introducing new routes. Transport for London owns many of the piers and is now considering how this could be integrated with a land-based public transport.

Operators of existing or failed services say that there are still difficulties in running the boats successfully. One of the biggest is propeller fouling. Although the river is much cleaner than twenty or thirty years ago a considerable amount of flotsam and jetsam is still on or close to the surface of the water and can easily get entwined with propellers. Fares have been quite high, reflecting high operating costs and many operators have found it difficult to get to that critical mass where they can provide a sufficiently frequent service to be attractive to busy commuters or business people who are short of time during the working day.

The Mayor also draws attention to the success of the Port of London handling 10.9 million tons of freight destined for use within Greater London in 1999. The Mayor is responsible for waste policy. Bulk transport by water is a very attractive and sensible option. It does not really matter how long it takes to get the waste to the processing plant or tip but it does matter how much it costs. The relative cheapness and slowness of water transport is ideally suited to waste material. Wharves within the Greater London Authority boundary predominantly handle household waste, aggregates and sugar. The aggregate movements alone on water remove the need for 430,000 lorry movements.

The Mayor's transport strategy is somewhat defensive seeking to keep open the wharves that already exist and prevent them from being redeveloped for other purposes. Again, we need a more ambitious strategy with the London authorities recognising the full potential of the river, once London's greatest highway.

London government, both national and local can certainly make maximum use of the river when procuring transport for bulk trades like waste disposal. The national and local government is a big user of construction materials in London. It has control over all road contracts and several large building projects. All these could have their materials sourced from waterborne transport.

The Thames is also a potential route for more cables, pipes and other means of communicating and transporting bulk fluids. There have been suggestions that a tunnel could be sunk onto the river bed and indented into the mud, the water pumped out and then London would have a new highway through the middle. This would be an expensive and more visionary project but it would be well worth looking again at its feasibility, given the chronic shortage of transport capacity throughout most of the metropolitan area.

Waterborne transport flourished for many years in the seventeenth and eighteenth centuries. It was eclipsed first by the railway and then the lorry and van. In our current crowded island we need to make maximum use of any network available. It is time to look again at the potential for waterborne transport and for new forms of transport using the wayleaves and routes that the coast, rivers and canals offer.

Third Way water transport is highly taxed, highly regulated and in the case of the canals, heavily subsidised. There is little point in promoting partnerships between different parts of the public sector for the canals; they would be better in the private sector. Coastal and ocean shipping is provided by free enterprise but they find tax and regulation unhelpful. It is time to let the market do more to promote this environmentally friendly way of transport.

Chapter nine

FLYING HIGH –
FREE ENTERPRISE TAKES TO THE SKIES

The aviation success story

AVIATION IS A GREAT SUCCESS story of the second half of the twentieth century. It was a luxury for the privileged few in the 1930's. Now air travel is the necessity of the many as we travel on holiday or business to a stunning array of destinations. The Heathrow grass strip of the early pioneering days of aviation has been turned into the world's busiest international airport. Some forty different airlines operate planes with twenty seats or more from around the United Kingdom. In recent years the competition has been intense, with the arrival on the scene of a series of low-cost airlines offering ever more capacity at still cheaper rates. In the 1930's most people would not have dreamt that they would be able to afford to fly. In the 1950's and 1960's many felt they might be able to fly once in a lifetime as a special treat. By the 1990's most families in the country anticipated flying several times in their lifetime and many decided on annual holidays by taking a low-cost or charter flight to a destination abroad. In 1990, British airports handled ninety million terminal passengers. By 2000, this had almost doubled to 161 million. Growth is likely to be rapid from here.

Heathrow is the dominant airport in the United Kingdom, accommodating 64 million of the 161.3 million passengers in the year 2000. Gatwick was the next busiest handling 31.9 million with Manchester, third at 18.4. The four major London airports of Gatwick, Heathrow, Luton and Stansted handled almost 115 million passengers in the year 2000 between them. Air cargo has also built up quite rapidly. In 1990, United Kingdom airports handled over 100 million tons. This doubled to more than 200 million by the year 2000.

British Airways remains the largest British carrier running a fleet of 235 aircraft in the year 2000. The next largest, the Manx and British Regional Group, was flying forty-nine aircraft and the third largest, British Midland, forty-five. KLM, Airtours, Britannia, British European and Virgin had just over thirty planes whilst a series of yet smaller companies like Brymon, City Flyer, Emerald, European Air Charter, Monarch and Atlantic Airlines operated with less than thirty each. Despite the heavy congestion in our skies and on the ground in our busiest airports, the last ten years have seen mercifully few crashes and fatalities. Only thirty people have died in fixed wing accidents involving UK registered aircraft in United Kingdom air space and just three more have died in accidents in UK registered aircraft in foreign air space in the 1990 to 2000 period. Air travel has shown the fastest growth of any type of travel in recent years with a dramatic reduction in fares and charges. It has been the safest means of travel when measured by fatalities in relation to distance travelled. How, then, has this industry been such a success story? Why did it not suffer like its rival, the railways, struggling with price, safety and attractiveness of the service? Why should so many people decide to increase their air travel whilst reducing their train travel? Why is Britain renowned as a worldwide centre for aviation but is no mecca when it comes to surface transportation?

Government policy towards aviation
In the last five years aviation has probably benefited from the absence of serious ministerial involvement. Whilst ministers have been meddling wildly in the railways and road transport they have had little to say or do when it comes to action in the air. There has been an atmosphere of dither concerning the government's aviation policy. This has been punctuated by the occasional consultation document and vaguely threatening speeches about the need to do something to curb the impact of too many flights upon the environment. The ten year transport plan had practically nothing to say about aviation policy in general and certainly answered none of the specific big questions such as, should airport slots be auctioned, should Heathrow Airport be expanded and should further taxes be placed on the industry to reflect its environmental costs? The government did issue an important consultation document entitled 'The Future of Aviation' in December 2000, that contained some very encouraging comments about the general attitude of the government towards this private sector success. In July 2002 it issued a wide-ranging consultation document on expanding airports.

The White Paper stated clearly: "the government has a general presumption in favour of liberalising aviation services. Increasing free and fair competition between airlines is the most effective way of securing benefits for consumers and promoting economic efficiency and innovation. Greater commercialisation, not only of airlines but also airports and air traffic control services, has given government's less direct control but a more important role in ensuring fair competition and maintaining standards".

This remarkable statement sets out a wholly admirable policy towards an important transport industry. Because governments of all persuasions have generally followed this attitude over the last twenty years the aviation industry has had more chance to succeed than the struggling railways. The Conservative government of 1979 to 1990, under Margaret Thatcher, drove through two most important privatisations. Firstly, they sold shares in the leading national airline British Airways. At the same time, new leadership of the airline, led by John King as Chairman with Colin Marshall as Chief Executive, transformed the prospects of a loss making, low morale, poor performing company into one that could claim to be the world's favourite.

The government followed this up by selling off the state owned airports, creating a new company called BAA plc out of the old British Airports Authority. Although it was disappointing at the time that the government decided to keep the London airports under common ownership, removing the scope for proper competition between Heathrow, Gatwick and Stansted, the transformation was nonetheless important. A fairly sleepy nationalised enterprise suddenly became galvanised to exploit the important franchise under its control and to make much greater use of its property assets. Shopping was expanded and improved, the quality of the passenger experience was greatly enhanced by renovation and expansion of the terminal areas and the airports rushed to catch up with the great surge in demand being generated by a more competitive airline industry.

The structure of the industry is extremely complex. It breaks all the rules of public sector exponents of clarity, planning and centralisation. It shows it is quite possible to carry out a very complex set of activities with a whole series of different owners, agents and regulators involved. To the passenger things normally appear seamless even though a very large number of different organisations are involved in the successful transit from the edge of the airport in one location, to the gates of the airport in another.

An air passenger usually buys a ticket through an independent broker or travel agent. The travel agent has access to information from the ticketing systems of a series of airlines, offering his customer a choice of time, place and price for the journey he wishes to carry out. In the case of the south eastern traveller wishing to go to a destination abroad there maybe a choice of which airport in London as well as time of day, type of ticket and fare. The journey may involve travelling on more than one airline but the travel agent or ticket issuer will issue a series of tickets in a ticket book and collect a single fare. The different airlines involved will receive a fair proportion of the total paid by the customer.

On arrival at the airport the passenger will be receiving a service from the company owning that airport and a series of other franchise holders who work closely with the BAA or the other airport freeholder. The passenger may well park his car in a National Car Park, paying a fee directly to NCP. He may then be taken in a courtesy bus to the terminal and may decide to go shopping in a series of franchised stores before checking in at his chosen airline. He will go through security and other checks carried out by the airport operator or their sub-contractor before waiting in the airline lounge or the general holding area for the departure of his aircraft. Once on board his plane, he will be under the control of airline staff on board who in turn will be directed by the airport authorities when the plane is taxiing for take off. Once airborne, the airline staff will be under the control of British operated airspace, directed by National Air traffic Services. At the edge of UK airspace, when undertaking an international journey, responsibility for the air route taken by the plane will be transferred to another national jurisdiction.

The pilot on board the plane will be trained by the chosen airline but licensed by UK regulatory authorities. A UK registered plane itself will have an air worthiness certificate issued in the United Kingdom and will be subject to periodic checks and a strenuous maintenance schedule. There is substantial safety regulation applying both to the technical and flying staff and to the aeroplane itself.

Planning problems

The problems for aviation are the problems of success. They occur mainly at the intersection of a successful competitive commercial industry with the government and the regulator. The biggest single problem that aviation has faced in Britain emerges from the planning system. Whilst most British people are keener and keener to use planes more frequently to travel on business and for pleasure, we are also understandably reluctant to have more air traffic movements over our heads and more surface transport to and from an airport anywhere near us. Because our planning process is geared to hear any possible objector at considerable length, the aviation industry has been dogged by enormous delays in reaching agreement on where additional runway and terminal capacity can be provided, especially in the congested south east of the country which generates so many of the demands for air travel.

Heathrow is a two-runway airport. When Gatwick was built to relieve some of the pressure a promise was made to the local community that it would only be a one-runway airport. As a result London then needed a third airport, based at Stansted, with a single runway. It is also becoming more dependent on Luton providing the fifth runway serving the Greater London conurbation. Schipol in Amsterdam and Charles De Gaulle in France have not faced the same planning constraints when seeking more runway capacity.

Heathrow has fought back from the constraints imposed by limited runway space by concentrating more of its air traffic movements on larger aircraft to maximise the number of passengers that can use its facilities. This has required a larger expansion of terminal capacity to handle the increased numbers of travellers. Even this has been fraught with planning difficulties. It took many years to get agreement for the construction of the much needed Terminal 4 at Heathrow airport in the 1990's, only to be followed by further delay in reaching agreement on Terminal 5 which is also now sorely needed. Where airports like Charles De Gaulle or Singapore, both successful international players, are keen to market and promote their activities, seeking to attract more airlines to use their facilities, Heathrow has for many years been in the position of having to turn airlines away. There is a long waiting list for slots at Heathrow Airport and fierce competition over the allocation of any slots that do become available for whatever reason.

Can you get to the airport on time?
The second series of problems for British aviation has come about owing to the poor performance of many of the surface transport links to our airports. Again, Heathrow has been under the most pressure. Two important decisions have been taken in the last twenty years that have provided some much needed relief. The first was the decision of London Underground and the government to extend the Piccadilly Line to include the four terminals at Heathrow. This has provided some much needed extra capacity for passengers to travel into the centre of London. Secondly the privatised railway has been able to provide the much-needed link from Heathrow to Paddington via the Great Western. This too has proved very popular with more passengers than it can absorb at busy times of day owing to the limitation of capacity on the Great Western Line itself. Road links into the airport are even more inadequate than the railway ones. The main access to Heathrow takes place through a two lane

only tunnel where four lanes are clearly needed. There have been some improvements to the access road to the M4 but the motorway itself is greatly overburdened and will need additional widening to accommodate growing airport traffic.

Is aviation the great polluter in the sky?

The third problem for aviation has arisen from growing doubts about its environmental acceptability. Most of the present government's work on aviation has been concerned with the impact it has upon the environment. The government is worried about emissions from the aircraft, aircraft noise, the noise emission and congestion arising from surface access to airports, the urbanisation resulting from airport development and the energy consumption and water quality impacts of airport activities. Although emissions from international aviation are not currently included with the Kyoto Protocol reductions in atmospheric pollution, the UK and other signatories are required to work to limit or reduce emissions through the International Civil Aviation Organisation. The government likes the idea of the 'polluter pays' principle, which means that the government receives in tax its view of the environmental costs imposed by the aviation industry. It is flirting with general taxation on aviation movements or on aviation kerosene. It does, however, accept that unless the taxes are very high they would be unlikely to have dramatic impacts upon the phenomenal growth in demand for air travel.

The aviation industry is naturally worried that, although the government from time to time praises the service the industry offers, the safety record of the industry and the jobs it creates at the principal airports around the country, the drift of government policy is towards taking regulatory and taxation measures designed to dampen demand or to shift activity away from Britain to less regulated and less highly taxed centres elsewhere. The United Kingdom, as a very open and, until recently, relatively low cost centre for aviation, has been very successful in attracting a great deal of footloose traffic. Britain has been the dominant port of arrival and embarkation for routes from Europe to the Americas and back. The government needs to be careful lest its enthusiasm for taxation and regulation starts to undermine the strength of this position.

In their December 2000 Paper, the government seemed quite proud of the leading position of the United Kingdom in world aviation. They explained that London's airports have achieved this because "the UK has an open economy and participates heavily in international trade. London is a major world city with a particularly strong position in the international financial sector...language, cultural and business affinities have encouraged particularly large flows of passengers between the UK and North America, for both business and leisure." The government draws attention to the range of competitive and efficient airlines in the UK in both scheduled and charter sectors and takes some pride in the rapid growth in low cost airlines. It accepts that Charles De Gaulle with three runways and Schipol with five have obvious planning advantages compared with Heathrow and Gatwick. Over the past twenty years the numbers of passengers carried into and out of UK airports has trebled and air transport movements and freight movements has more than doubled. They expect something like 4% per annum compound growth over the next ten years, producing a further staggering increase in likely passenger numbers and freight movements. Low cost airlines have been growing their passenger numbers at an amazing 15% per year in recent years and the government anticipates that this is going to continue. This could of course be stopped it in its tracks by imposing substantial taxation and regulatory costs upon such airlines but the government is so far hesitating over doing so.

What should the government do?

The government should accept that aviation is a British success story and that more and more British people will wish to undertake more and more travel by plane. The government should of course be determined to keep up the very high standards of safety, supervised by a strong regulatory structure that is already in place. They should ensure that when planning for the growth they make the best possible decisions about the impact on the environment whilst offering compensation for those who will be adversely affected. The government should be worried about the impact of noise and atmospheric pollution and seek, by international agreement, to produce increasingly stringent standards worldwide that bear down on both problems. It makes no sense to impose especially tight regulations on British registered planes if all it succeeds in doing is transferring passengers and freight to less highly regulated airlines elsewhere. We belong to one world and it would be no advantage to see more KLM flights into Schipol polluting the atmosphere instead of BA flights into Heathrow.

The government needs to take important decisions quickly to raise the capacity of the airport system in general and the London airport system in particular. London certainly needs the fifth terminal which the government has now indicated it will accept. London will also need an additional runway to accommodate the great growth in plane movements without jeopardising safety. The only way this could now be achieved would be to pay substantial compensation to people living anywhere near such a new construction given the past promises made at both Heathrow and Gatwick.

The annoyance of additional runway and terminal capacity can be reduced by taking stringent action on noise. People will not accept night flights, even with reduced noise from quieter engines. There does have to be a quiet period during the twenty-four hours when people can have uninterrupted sleep. The government also needs to offer leadership worldwide to lower the maximum permitted noise levels for planes and to encourage early scrapping of noisy aircraft to make the whole experience more tolerable for those on the ground.

The government needs to make urgent and crucial decisions about surface transport to and from the airports. Heathrow itself needs both more road and rail capacity to handle the likely increase in passenger numbers that will wish to use the airport over the next twenty years. The government will need to widen and improve the junctions on the A4 near Heathrow as well as widening the M4 and the M25 in its western section. It will need to provide more direct road communication into the heart of the airport and ensure that there is good access to the new Terminal 5. It will need to allow more capacity to be included on the Great Western railway line into Paddington and should support the cross-rail project which should provide still more railway capacity from Heathrow across London with suitable stopping points along the way. Signalling and train upgrades on the Piccadilly Line could also result in more trains per hour being run on that line. Each of these public transport facilities needs to have better accommodation for travellers' luggage than is currently the case.

Should the government auction airport slots?

As Heathrow is such a congested airport there have been many arguments between carriers over who should enjoy the privilege of landing and taking off there. Under the current arrangements the existing carriers have 'grandfather rights'. It is quite difficult for a new challenger to get the slots needed to run a regular service and quite difficult for a medium sized competitor to grow into a large company operating out of Heathrow given the restrictions upon the availability of capacity to accommodate that growth.

There can be a shortage not only of runway capacity but also terminal capacity and a shortage of stands for people to get on and off the aircraft, into and out of the terminal building. Lack of runway space is the most frequent cause of carrier frustration but at Heathrow, elements of all three shortages occur, particularly at the busy times of the day. Returned or unused slots are placed in a pool and allocated according to administrative criteria. About half the pool of available slots is reserved for new entrants usually only assisting very small carriers offering low frequency services. A current user of the slot has the right to use it in perpetuity, subject only to a use it or lose it obligation. This means that large carriers can keep control of a large number of slots even when they find it difficult to put them to good commercial use. It makes sense for them in these circumstances to run very small aircraft at a loss offering relatively unpopular services just to keep the slot until better times return, allowing them to put on a large plane flying to a popular destination to make decent money. This has led the government to consider auctioning of slots.

They were greatly encouraged by the success of their auction of spectrum for the telecommunications industry which did undeniably raise a very large sum of money for the taxpayer by selling something to the telephone companies that had previously been available free. Unfortunately, this experience turned out to be part of the reason why the telecoms industry entered an extremely difficult period with several companies needing re-financing or going bankrupt. The auction was designed to maximise the price the telecoms companies had to offer to stay in business. They duly responded, bidding an astonishing £22,000 million for the licences to run mobile telephone services. The German government followed suit and raised an additional £28,000 million from the same industry. Shortly afterwards a number of large telephone companies had to admit that they had run out of money, were unable to build up their networks in the way they wished and had to sell assets, raise money from shareholders and banks or put themselves into administration.

None of this damage is reflected in the government's thinking or in the report it commissioned from DotEcon Ltd, published in January 2001. The consultants concluded "market based mechanisms such as auctions have substantial advantages over administrative procedures ... any revenues raised from a slot auction reflect excess profits that operators would otherwise earn if allocated a slot for free. To the extent the competition in air services markets will be expected to be vigorous, there will be low willingness to pay for slots and low prices". This seems to be whistling in the wind after the experience of the telecoms industry.

The government took clever mathematical advice on the design of the telecoms auction. Knowing that there was likely to be at least one more bidder than there were licences available, the government agreed to a scheme that entailed re-bidding over many rounds to drive the price ever higher. Each board of directors reasoned that it had to stay in the business of mobile telephony and that to stay in the business it needed to have one of the elusive licences. Each business ended up paying a very high price with no immediate prospect of getting that money back from customers but decided they had to do it in order to stay trading in their chosen area of activity. If there is artificial scarcity in supply the price achieved will be greater than the excess profits.

The same could happen with the auction of slots. The airline industry at the moment is in dire financial straits. The 11 September 2001 tragedy in New York led to a sharp downturn in air travel especially in lucrative trans-Atlantic travel which has greatly weakened the revenue accounts and the balance sheets of the major airlines of the world. If they now had to bid to continue with the routes they are currently running they would be badly torn. Many boards of directors would probably conclude that they just had to bid a high price in order to stay in their chosen line of business and have a chance of using the planes they have bought at considerable expense, even though their calculations would tell them that they could not afford the financial price. It is not good regulatory practice to pose leading players in an industry with an insoluble dilemma. If they do not bid they go out of business because they can no longer fly their planes. If they do bid because the number of slots is inadequate for all of the airlines wishing to use them they will end up having to pay too much in order to secure the slots. All that the auction will prove, as the auction for too few licences for radio telephony proved, is that if you artificially restrict the supply of a good like airspace or landing slots you will drive its price to absurdly high levels.

The consultants do foresee other problems when designing a slot auction. Although they regard the radio spectrum auction as a success, they do see that an airline participating in a slot auction is going to want not just the right to use a runway but also the related opportunities. It would be no good auctioning the right to runway space at particular times of the day if the airline then discovered it could not get a stand and sufficient terminal capacity at that time. As the consultants rightly conclude, it would be best to group the runway landing right with the stand and the terminal capacity and make the bids conditional upon all three being available.

There is an added hazard in airport slot auctions. It is no good having a right to take off from Heathrow at a stated time unless the airline also has an equivalent right to land at the airport of its choice at the relevant time of arrival. Similarly there is no point having a landing time and right at Heathrow unless the airline has an equivalent take off right and time for the service it plans. The consultants conclude: "UK airport slots need to be matched with corresponding slots at other airports. Hence, any UK auction would need to be compatible with the IATA procedures and timetable for international slot co-ordination. Realistically an auction must be completed within a period of a few weeks." If, of course, the UK adopted slot auctions and other European jurisdictions followed suit it could become an extremely difficult game for an airline faced with the need to bid at both ends of the route. It would need to secure the exact slot at the other airport to gain any value from the slot it had already secured at Heathrow following the first auction.

The consultants point out that where US airports have introduced market mechanisms it has resulted in increased concentration of slot holding. American Airlines have decided to make one particular airport their hub or centre. The prices have not been too high and the market damage this has caused has not been very great because of the relatively plentiful supply of runway and terminal capacity in the United States. There are many large cities in the United States offering good airport services without the same planning controls that have bedevilled Heathrow and Gatwick. The consultants argue that a system has to be found to prevent British Airways, for example, deciding to make Heathrow its hub and bidding enough to buy up all the slots it needs to do so. It would not be easy inventing such a rule. The current pattern of usage shows that BA is a most important player at Heathrow. The design of the slot auction could make or break the airline on its own.

The consultants also recognise that there are a number of routes from Heathrow and Gatwick to the UK regions that might not meet the market test. They suggest that to combat this problem the taxpayer and government would need to subsidise the airlines and the bidding so that the regional routes remained open regardless of the price. For example, BA might decide that it was not worthwhile running a Heathrow to Belfast service if it had to pay a higher price for the slot. It would be difficult for the government to prevent BA making commercial decisions on its routes but would be equally embarrassing for the government if an important link between

London and Belfast was severed as a result of a government decision to go for a more commercial approach to slot allocation.

The government is advised to auction usage rights lasting between three and six years. The consultants optimistically say, "Relatively short tenures on slots have the additional advantage of lowering the likely price of slots and reducing financing requirements. This may provide encouragement to smaller carriers and entrants". The alternative way of looking at it is that offering such short tenure on slots could put people off running services at all. No businessman is going to want to buy aircraft, invest a lot of money in building up a particular route over a three to six year period only to discover that a competitor decides that it would be a good idea to wreck that particular service by bidding a high price at the auction for the slot. The government would be wise to temper this advice with some understanding of the amount of activity, investment and effort needed to build up a particular route or service and to see that the investment might need carrying over a longer period than three to six years.

The consultants rightly see that a secondary market would be needed to allow for changes for airlines' circumstances and service usage patterns between auctions. The company which had bid too much and picked up too many slots would certainly need an opportunity to relieve itself of some of the burden by selling the excess ones for whatever it could achieve. Similarly, companies driven into bankruptcy perhaps by the auction process itself as with the telecoms industry, would like to know that their administrative receiver could at least sell on the slots to reduce the pain to shareholders and bankers.

The consultants do not come up with any simple device for preventing one powerful airline cornering the market in an auction. They give as an example the idea of a quantitative limit but suggest it is too blunt an instrument. They suggest instead developing some anti-competition rule which they have not yet developed fully. They also suggest that if auctions were introduced smaller carriers could hold slots they were not using. This would make sense if there were enough slots available but it does not seem a good idea where the underlying problem is one of an acute shortage of slots at the popular airports. Their conclusion that we might need a European-wide regime to do what they want to do is not surprising. It would be even better to have a worldwide regime dealing with the principal regulatory issues as people wish to fly from Heathrow to the other four continents of the world as well as to Europe.

Euro Control

European jurisdiction is becoming more and more important in the aviation field. There are moves now to create a common European airspace and a common European regulator over it. The European Court of Human Rights has become involved in the issue of night flying. In a landmark decision it determined in October 2001 that the loss of sleep suffered by residents under Heathrow's flight paths violated their human rights. The Court ruled 5:2 that the British government had breached Article 8 of the European Convention because "the state failed to strike a fair balance between the United Kingdom's economic well being and the applicants' effective enjoyment of their right to respect to their homes and their private and family lives". The judges also said that Britain had breached Article 13 by not offering sufficient redress for residents under British law for their human rights. The Court has subsequently decided to consider an appeal as the government has complained that ministers do deserve some discretion in this respect.

The United Kingdom needs to be careful if it wishes to protect and enhance the lead that British aviation has compared with continental competitors. If it signs up to a common European airspace and to more European control over flight paths and routes it will also lead to European control over airport developments and slot allocation. It might be more rational from the Europe wide perspective, to make more use of the additional runway capacity already available at Charles De Gaulle and Schipol than to allow or encourage the construction of new capacity at Heathrow or Gatwick. Whilst this would be welcomed by noise protesters living adjacent to Heathrow or Gatwick it would greatly inconvenience the travelling public in Britain who would then need to undertake short haul hops to Charles De Gaulle or Schipol before transferring to inter-continental flights. It would be damaging to job prospects, particularly in the south east around the successful airports in the London area.

The government is committed to playing a prominent role in Euro Control. Euro Control, the European organisation for the safety of air navigation wishes to co-ordinate and harmonise European air traffic management more effectively. The government supports the EU's accession to Euro Control to maximise "political, economic, legal and social influences in favour of strengthening and reforming the organisation". The European Union's communication entitled 'Single European Sky' was presented to the Transport Council of the EU in December 1999. The government is playing a dangerous game in encouraging stronger EU involvement in this area. The EU in itself is not the only interested party in European airspace, given the non-membership of the EU by countries like Norway and Switzerland, as well as all of the countries to the east of Germany and Austria. The government should be aware that more European Union control over Euro Control might lead to majority decisions that did not favour the development of more aviation based in the United Kingdom.

The curious case of National Air Traffic Services: "Our air is not for sale"

Until 1997 it was common ground between the two main political parties in Britain, the Conservatives and Labour, that air traffic control in Britain should be provided by a public sector regulatory monopoly body under the control of the Civil Aviation Authority. The Civil Aviation Authority had a range of functions of a regulatory nature running air traffic control as well as being responsible for airworthiness, pilot licensing, economic regulation and general safety. The Conservatives decided against the privatisation of the CAA in general and National Air Traffic Services in particular on the grounds that it was a regulatory monopoly and not one that could be easily split or made competitive. The Labour party in opposition echoed this by assuring the public, "Our air is not for sale" in the famous words of Andrew Smith who subsequently became Chief Secretary to the Treasury. Labour thought the Conservatives might get round to privatising air traffic services and felt that this would be unpopular with the public. It never looked likely that the Conservatives would actually carry this out, having rejected it continuously during their eighteen years in office.

In July 1999, the government made a most surprising decision. It decided that National Air Traffic Services should be completely separated from the Civil Aviation Authority and should be re-established as a so-called 'public private partnership'. They were persuaded that the air traffic control system in Britain was out of date and required substantial further investment to modernise it fully. It was undeniably true that the system needed extra capacity to handle the phenomenal growth that we are experiencing. The sums of money were not large by public expenditure standards. However, the government decided that it was a suitable case for treatment where private sector involvement could relieve the Treasury of the cost burden and where it might also bring improved management. They stated that the aim of the PPP was "to deliver a safe, modern and efficient air traffic control system...it would do this by giving it enhanced investment and project management skills as well as greater access to private capital for investment. This, in turn, should provide a platform for the NATS PPP to exploit some of the opportunities that are expected to emerge internationally, exploiting its expertise abroad and expanding into new markets".

In practice, although it was called a PPP, the government had designed a privatisation and had put forward the classic case for a privatisation. All privatisations set out to liberate the management, raise much more private capital than can be provided in the public sector and offer the opportunity of sales and expansion abroad. One of the common characteristics of Britain's nationalised industries in the post-war period was their unwillingness or their inability to undertake abroad what they were doing at home. The national public monopolies looked in on themselves. They claimed the Treasury blocked them from raising capital to expand abroad but they were never very keen to do so given the relatively comfortable positions they had at home drawing monopoly money from the paying public and topping it up with subsidy from the taxpayer should the need arise.

Labour's left was far from happy with the decision to go for a public private partnership for National Air Traffic Services. They conjured up the possibility that a PPP would be far less safe for the travelling public than the public monopoly it was replacing. They seemed less concerned about the possibility of exerting monopoly power over the airlines using the service and were reassured on any fears they may have had in this connection when a consortium of airlines announced that they wished to be one of the main bidders.

When the competition was completed the government adjudged the airline consortium the winners. The state maintained a 49% holding, 5% was sold to the employees of National Air Traffic Services and the remaining 46% transferred to the airline consortium. Statements were made about controlling the level of charges NATS could impose and money was raised from the transaction to expand the investment made in improving the systems. Selling such a large minority to the airlines was an extraordinary thing to do, making the risk of failure more likely given the financial weakness and cyclical nature of that industry.

Unfortunately for the government, shortly after all this had been completed terrorists decided to blow up the twin towers of the World Trade Centre in New York. The resulting collapse in trans-Atlantic flying led to a sharp reduction in revenues for National Air

Traffic Services as flights were cancelled and passenger numbers plummeted. Private sector buyers, the airlines, suffered badly in their principal lines of business as full fare passengers cancelled or proved elusive. At the same time, NATS needed more money to keep going as its own revenue account had been damaged by the decline in the number of flights. As a result shortly after the triumphant announcement of the PPP another statement had to be made that it had needed refinancing early on its life. It had been revealed that allowing the main customers to become the principal shareholders had its drawbacks when a volatile industry like aviation hit major turbulence financially with a sharp decline in fare revenue.

The safety of our air traffic control system will be as dependent in the future as it was under complete public ownership on the quality of the staff and on the success of the computerised programme, largely set up before the privatisation. Safety has not been endangered by the privatisation itself. We can only trust that the standards in the future will be as high as they have proved to be in the past in keeping British airspace relatively free of incidents and remarkably free, in recent years, of major tragedies.

The decision to privatise NATS is all of a piece with a government determined to show in the field of aviation that free markets, private capital, and competition are best. Although the government has proved unable to create competitive forces in air traffic control services for obvious reasons it did have a competition of sorts to arrange the shareholding and financing. Its general policy remains enamoured with the forces of the market and most of its statements on aviation are looking for ways to strengthen competitive forces in the airline industry which is a good thing.

Future problems with the government's approach

The danger in the government's approach from the point of view of the successful further development of our aviation services lies in two respects. The first is that the government seems very keen for the European authorities to play a bigger and bigger role in the regulation of airspace which will lead on to more general regulation and taxation powers. The second is the government's own belief, perhaps influenced by the way of European thinking generally, that aviation is by nature an environmentally damaging activity. It seems to believe it needs restrictive regulation to limit the numbers of people using the service and higher taxation to provide a cost and price disincentive, as well as some kind of punishment to those who choose to make their living by flying people around the world.

The government's approach is contradictory. It does not take a similar attitude towards the pollution coming out of the back of old buses or to the pollution from diesel multiple units on the railways. Nor does it apparently see the innate contradiction between its wish to have a competitive, expanding aviation sector with more and more people offered the chance of cheap flights on the one hand and on the other its wish to regulate and tax which will make operating these low cost airlines more and more difficult out of a British base.

The government will be well advised to see the need for a global approach to aviation strategy. It will get a better deal if it negotiates internationally rather than just in the European context. Britain is an important staging post between the new and the old world and we need to fight to protect our position as the biggest port of arrival and embarkation for the United States. Britain can be, given the strength of its global aviation position, one of the leaders in seeking benign or common regulation on a worldwide basis.

Of course we should do more to limit the noise and pollution damage brought about by planes. The best way of doing this is to set ever higher standards for noise and pollution control for each generation of new jets and to encourage airlines to buy new ones as quickly as possible. This will not be achieved by introducing slot auctions and higher taxes. This will damage the cash flow of airlines further, making it more difficult for them to afford the new generations of planes which could deliver the higher environmental standards. We need to make sure these standards are imposed globally to have the impact we want on the worldwide pollution problem and to make sure that British aviation does not suffer from UK or European penalties. The government needs to make early decisions about where it will allow new runway and terminal capacity to be built in the South-East to cater for the likely large increase in demand. Aviation is a UK success story so far. Its success stems from our reliance on free enterprise, competition and choice.

Conclusions

THERE IS NO MAGIC MONEY. The story of Third Way finance has been a fascinating kaleidoscope of explanations and devices as the Government has turned this way and that to find off balance sheet money to buttress Britain's ageing transport systems.

Analysis of the arguments and results so far shows that there does need to be a clear segregation of risk to make private finance worthwhile. The private sector can undoubtedly do more; the public sector should do less. The private sector should build the boats and run the engines; the public sector can signal a course and supervise the flotilla.

Competition usually brings better performance. The Government agrees about this in the case of aviation where it speaks up for more consumer choice and basks in the warm glow of more services and lower fares brought about by more competition. Yet, when it comes to airports, the Government perseveres with monopoly ownership of the two main London airports and continues to restrict the provision of new capacity, preventing choice and competition lowering charges and improving airports.

The Government does not favour competition when it comes to railways. They are resolutely against breaking the track monopoly given to Railtrack although they favour different ownership of this monopoly. They wish to restrict choice and competition amongst train companies inventing the strange doctrine that there should be only one operating company using each London terminus. Surely if competition brings lower fares and better service in the skies, as it does, so competition could bring lower fares and better choice on the tracks? The mistake at privatisation was not to encourage more train companies but to leave in place too many monopoly elements which limited the scope for improvement in overall service levels.

Nor does the Government favour competition when it comes to the provision of road space. Instead of allowing private contractors to build new toll roads to make up for the chronic lack of capacity in the free monopoly public system, the Government has cut back the road-building programme further. As a result, the motoring public and the freight carriers are left feeling very unhappy about the difficulty of making the journeys they wish to make. We are short of railway track, roads and airport space, which are all supplied by effective monopolies.

The attempt to find a Third Way between outright public

ownership and free enterprise has been particularly pronounced in transport and particularly unsuccessful. When the Government began, the railways and London Underground were entirely in public ownership along with the canals and the roads. The regulated airspace was controlled in the public sector but railways, airports, civil aviation and road transport were all privately owned. The areas in free enterprise competition were growing rapidly and were popular. The areas under the control of public monopoly were in decline and were unpopular.

There has been no clear pattern to this Government's policies. The previous Government placed air travel, airports, and railways in the private sector through privatisation. It did not nationalise anything. This Government has placed railways into receivership en route to accepting many of the liabilities of this mode of travel. It has put air traffic services into the private sector and has tried to construct a halfway house for the tube through the PPP. Supporters would say this shows how balanced and pragmatic the policy has been. Critics say it shows great muddle, with a fruitless search for a halfway house that does not exist. Something is either in the private sector or there is recourse to the taxpayer.

The Government has continued the policy of charging users directly for rail, tube and canal travel but imposing taxes to provide a road network. The logic of its position, wishing to curb car use, should be to impose charges for the use of the roads rather than taxing people for owning a car in the first place. After much debate about so-called congestion charging, making motorists pay for the inadequacy of the roads provided, there has still been no actual imposition of such charges on any British road. The Government is obviously worried about the unpopularity of such a move.

Perhaps it is time to allow toll roads to be constructed to ease the capacity shortage whilst making users of the better facilities pay directly for them. It is right to continue to charge train and bus users for the service provided, although there is a worrying build up of subsidy levels as the Government and nationalised travel providers decide to offer services which are not popular enough to be self-financing.

I have shown how competition could be introduced into railways, canals and waterways, the tube and road provision. I have shown how the British Waterways Board could be privatised, new private toll roads constructed, the tube turned into the Londoner's tube, co-owned by all Londoners and commuters, and Railtrack returned again fully and properly to the private sector. This would provide a platform for a massive expansion of investment in the transport networks we need.

It is a salutary thought that all, bar one, of the great transport networks in this country were built originally with private capital through competing companies. The trunk roads were tolled turnpikes. The canals were all privately financed, as were the railways. Only the motorway network was constructed with taxpayers' money, and that remains too small and incomplete. It has fallen foul of budget cuts and political fashion long before motorways could be superseded by something better.

If we want environmentally friendly transport, including expanded rail, tube and waterway routes, it is going to take free enterprise capital to do it. Third Way finance is a move towards proper private finance but it still leaves the public sector with too much risk and too little reward. We need more cross-Channel rail links and Dartford crossings which show what private capital can do when given its head. All the tube PPP is likely to do is to leave us with a big bill for the taxpayer and a tube struggling to keep up.

In a relatively small and crowded island we need to be careful with the environment. All types of motorised transport, buses and trains as well as cars and lorries, emit too many unpleasant substances from their exhausts. Cutting the age of the vehicle fleet is the best way of reducing emissions as new engines are much cleaner than old ones. Tax incentives should be given to help achieve this. Providing more capacity on the roads and railways can also help, far more fumes are emitted if vehicles are kept waiting with engines running or if there is slow moving traffic brought about by congestion. Tax incentives for cleaner performance, coupled with removing capacity bottlenecks, could make a big impact on the environmental problem.

In a relatively rich society we need to accept that people do want to travel around. With both husband and wife usually working it will not be possible for both to live near to their jobs, so there will be requirements for travel to work. People want to travel to good sporting and leisure events, to the best shopping centres and to see friends and relatives. We need to accommodate these demands for travel using the trains for the popular routes at busy times of the day and the roads for other more difficult journeys.

All this requires more capacity of all kinds, which in turn requires more private capital. The tube PPP shows just how expensive it can be to raise modest sums of money from the private sector if the public sector insists on making many of the important decisions. The National Air Traffic Services PPP has shown how a misjudged version will soon result in the taxpayer being asked to put up more money to handle a problem that the private sector would handle under proper privatisation. Third Way finance is expensive money. Many of the projects will come bouncing back to the Government to sort out as insufficient risk has been transferred. If the Government wishes to call the tune it has to pay the piper. If it wishes to get rid of the risk then it has to do what it did some years ago with aviation and sell out completely, allowing the private sector to take the strains. We are likely to discover in the years ahead that the taxpayer would have been better off with direct public finance for the tube and railways, given the terms of the deals this Government has drawn up. Transport will remain a crucial battleground in the years to come between those who want more private enterprise and those who want more nationalisation. Both sides will end up agreeing that the Third Way was an expensive irrelevance, a muddle in the middle, a crazy presentational idea that was never going to work in practice. I come not to praise the Third Way, but to help bury it decently.

Appendix 1

Table 1: Relative emission performance of different vehicle types by fuel and emission standard of an urban test cycle[13]

Type of Vehicle	Emission Standard	Carbon Monoxide	Hydro- Carbons	Oxides of Nitrogen	Particulates
Petrol car	pre-Euro I	100	100	100	5
	Euro I	15	9	19	2
	Euro II	10	4	9	2
	Euro III	7	3	6	2
	Euro IV	4	2	3	2
Diesel Car	pre-Euro I	7	10	43	100
	Euro I	4	4	29	55
	Euro II	3	3	21	31
	Euro III	2	2	13	20
	Euro IV	2	1	7	10
Petrol LGV	pre-Euro I	151	120	114	10
	Euro I	30	6	21	5
	Euro II	21	3	9	5
	Euro III	17	2	6	5
	Euro IV	7	1	3	5
Diesel LGV	pre-Euro I	10	20	82	209
	Euro I	8	15	40	115
	Euro II	6	9	30	63
	Euro III	4	4	26	41
	Euro IV	3	3	13	20
Rigid HGV	pre-Euro I	38	192	640	484
	Euro I	21	113	440	318
	Euro II	17	105	316	168
	Euro III	9	45	224	113
	Euro IV	6	33	158	22
Articulated HGV	pre-Euro I	44	183	1704	700
	Euro I	22	87	893	482
	Euro II	18	78	650	185
	Euro III	9	47	461	124
	Euro IV	7	33	325	24
Bus	pre-Euro I	63	83	795	458
	Euro I	28	90	859	304
	Euro II	22	84	614	187
	Euro III	11	50	436	125
	Euro IV	8	35	307	24
Motorcycle	less than 50cc: two stroke	34	135	2	-
	greater than 50cc: two stroke	74	338	4	-
	greater than 50cc: four stroke	67	68	13	-

[13] Emission performance indexed to petrol car without three way catalyst (Pre-Euro 1 = 100), except for particulates where it is indexed to pre-Euro 1 diesel car. Legislative standards for particulates exist only for diesel vehicles. Petrol figures included for comparison. Motorcycles are not subject to Euro standards.

Source: Environmental impacts of road vehicles in use July 1999 Department of the Environment Transport and the Regions.

Please note that these tables are reproduced from original sources and we are therefore not responsible for any inaccuracies.

Appendix 2

Waterborne transport within the United Kingdom, 1990 – 2000

a) Goods lifted	1990	1991	1992	1993	1994	1995	1996	1997	1998	1999	2000
Coastwise										million tonnes	
Liquid bulks [1]	43.8	43.9	42.6	42.4	43.2	48.9	53.9	52.4	55.3	52.2	42.6
Coal	3.4	4.0	3.8	2.6	2.4	3.6	1.5	1.8	1.8	1.3	1.3
Other	14.3	15.2	15.7	15.2	15.5	15.2	15.5	16.9	20.2	19.5	19.2
Total	61.4	63.1	62.0	60.2	61.2	67.7	70.9	71.1	77.3	73.0	63.1
One-port											
From rigs [1]	14.1	13.2	13.2	10.4	14.1	10.1	8.1	5.1	10.3	14.3	50.1
To rigs	4.4	3.8	4.0	3.8	3.2	3.1	3.6	4.0	3.7	3.7	1.7
Sea dredged	19.5	15.2	13.9	12.5	13.9	14.6	13.0	13.6	14.2	14.8	11.9
Sea dumped	11.2	11.0	10.7	10.0	8.9	8.7	8.8	8.7	4.5	0.5	-
Total	49.2	43.1	41.7	36.7	40.1	36.4	33.5	31.3	32.6	33.3	63.7
Inland waters											
Internal	6.0	5.4	5.9	6.4	7.1	6.6	5.7	4.8	4.3	4.3	4.3
Coastwise	13.0	12.7	12.3	11.6	11.2	9.0	9.3	8.2	9.6	8.7	9.3
Foreign	35.6	32.5	29.6	31.2	32.1	32.7	32.0	34.6	35.3	33.9	30.8
One-port	14.8	12.5	12.1	10.5	11.6	12.5	10.2	10.9	8.2	7.0	4.5
Total	69.3	63.1	59.9	59.5	61.9	60.7	57.2	58.5	57.3	53.8	49.0
Overall [1 2]	152.1	144.2	139.2	134.3	140.4	143.4	142.1	141.8	149.4	144.5	161.9

b) Goods moved	1990	1991	1992	1993	1994	1995	1996	1997	1998	1999	2000
Coastwise										billion tonne-kilometres	
Liquid bulks [1]	32.1	31.2	29.4	28.9	28.7	33.1	38.7	33.8	36.5	33.1	27.6
Coal	1.4	1.8	1.7	1.5	1.2	2.3	0.6	0.6	0.5	0.5	0.2
Other	4.8	7.7	7.5	6.2	5.2	5.3	5.9	5.9	7.7	6.8	8.7
Other domestic [3]	0.2	0.2	0.2	0.2	0.2	0.3	0.3	0.2	0.3	0.2	-
Total	38.4	40.9	38.8	36.7	35.4	41.0	45.4	40.4	45.0	40.6	36.5
One-port											
From rigs [1]	12.9	13.0	12.5	11.0	13.3	8.7	6.5	4.2	8.6	14.8	53.4
To rigs	0.8	0.7	0.7	0.7	0.6	0.6	0.7	0.7	0.6	0.7	1.7
Sea dredged	0.9	0.7	0.6	0.5	0.6	0.7	0.6	0.6	0.6	0.7	0.8
Sea dumped	0.2	0.2	0.2	0.2	0.2	0.2	0.2	0.2	0.1	-	-
Other domestic [3]	0.1	0.1	0.1	0.1	0.1	-	-	-	-	-	-
Total	14.9	14.7	14.1	12.5	14.7	10.2	7.9	5.7	10.0	16.2	56.0
Inland waters											
Internal	0.2	0.2	0.2	0.2	0.2	0.2	0.2	0.2	0.2	0.2	0.2
Coastwise	0.4	0.4	0.4	0.3	0.3	0.2	0.2	0.2	0.2	0.2	0.2
Foreign	1.2	1.1	1.0	1.1	1.1	1.2	1.2	1.3	1.3	1.3	1.0
One-port	0.6	0.5	0.5	0.4	0.4	0.3	0.3	0.3	0.3	0.3	0.2
Total	2.4	2.1	2.0	2.0	2.1	1.9	1.9	1.9	2.0	1.9	1.7
Overall [1 2]	55.7	57.5	54.9	51.2	52.2	53.1	55.3	48.1	56.9	58.7	93.8

[1] More accurate recording of the origin and destination of crude oil traffic in 2000 has meant that 2000 figures for coastwise and one-port traffic are not directly comparable with previous years. In addition in 2000, one-port oil includes shipments of crude oil from North Sea oil fields in foreign sectors.

[2] The 'Overall tonnages' in table 1 (a) for all years and in table 1 (b) for 2000 are calculated by the addition of the totals for coastwise traffic, one-port traffic, and the internal and foreign components of inland waters traffic.

[3] 'Other domestic' refers to short penetrations of inland waters by coastwise or one-port traffic until 1999.

Please note that these tables are reproduced from original sources and we are therefore not responsible for any inaccuracies.

Waterborne transport within the United Kingdom by cargo category, 2000

Billion tonne-kilometres

Cargo category	On inland waters [1]				At sea [1]		Total
	Internal	Coastwise	Foreign	One-port	Coastwise	One-port [2]	
Crude petroleum and petroleum products	-	0.2	0.2	-	27.5	53.3	81.2
Ores	-	-	-	-	-	-	0.0
Coal	-	-	-	-	0.2	-	0.2
Agricultural products	-	-	0.1	-	0.5	-	0.6
Other dry bulk	0.2	0.1	0.2	0.2	5.6	0.7	6.9
Unitised	-	-	0.3	-	2.3	-	2.5
Forestry products	-	-	0.1	-	0.1	-	0.1
Iron and steel products	-	-	0.1	-	-	0.3	0.4
Other cargo	-	-	-	-	0.1	1.5	1.7
Total	0.2	0.2	1.0	0.2	36.3	55.8	93.8

[1] To avoid double counting, the inland waters components of coastwise and one-port traffics have been excluded from the 'At sea' category.
[2] Includes shipments of crude oil from North Sea oil fields in foreign sectors.

Freight transport in the United Kingdom, percentage by mode, 2000

(Note: Water includes shipments of crude oil from North Sea oil fields in foreign sectors)

	Pipeline	Water	Rail	Road
Goods lifted	7%	8%	5%	80%
Goods moved	4%	33%	6%	57%

Please note that these tables are reproduced from original sources and we are therefore not responsible for any inaccuracies.

Glossary of terms

Amersham International Government laboratory privatised in 1882

Apollo US manned lunar programme (1963-1972)

Associated British Ports Statutory corporation established under the Transport Act (1981) to administer ports previously administered by British Transport Dock Board

BAA plc British Airports Authority

BBC British Broadcasting Corporation

Beeching Dr Richard Beeching, Chairman of British Railways Board 1963

Birt, Sir John Tony Blair's strategy advisor and former Chairman of the BBC

Bletchley Park World War II establishment responsible for deciphering the 'Enigma' codes

BOAC British Overseas Airways Corporation, now part of British Airways

Bowker, Richard Chairman of the Strategic Rail Authority

BP British Petroleum

British Aerospace Manufacturers of defence weapons and aeronautics

British Caledonian Airline formed in 1970 from the merger of Caledonian Airways and British United Airways

British Leyland Car manufacturing company created from the merger of British Motor Corporation and Leyland Motors in the 1960's

British Shipping: Charting a new course White Paper on the future of shipping published December 1998

British Telecom Privatised telecommunications company established in 1984

British Waterways Organisation responsible for the running and conservation of all British waterways

BritOil Formerly British National Oil Corporation

BT Bonds Issued by British Telecom in 2001

Bullet Train Pioneering Japanese high-speed train

BWB British Waterways Board

Byers, Stephen Secretary of State for Transport, June 2001 to May 2002

Carlisle State Brewery State-owned brewery privatised in the 1970's

Channel Tunnel rail link Rail link under English Channel opened in May 1994

Civil Aviation Authority National air regulator

CO2 emissions Carbon dioxide emissions

Consignia Owns Royal Mail, Post Office and Post Office worldwide

Cross-channel rail link Channel Tunnel rail link due to be completed 2006

Cross-Rail London cross-rail link between Paddington and Liverpool Street Stations

Devil's Punch Bowl Area of outstanding beauty and scientific interest on the Surrey/ Hampshire Border.

DotEcon report January 2001 Airport slots auction feasibility study

DTLR Department of Transport, Local Government and the Regions

East London Line Project developed by London Underground Limited to improve access between East London and Central London

Ernst and Young International professional services organisation

EU European Union

Euro Control Europe's air navigation system

Fairey Manufacturing company, changed its name to Spectris in 2001

Falkirk Wheel First rotating boatlift

Ferranti Pioneering British computer company

Future of Aviation 2000 Consultation document published in December 2000, concerned with environmental issues, noise and the future of air transport

GLA Greater London Authority

Grandfather rights Rights which, in this instance, allow airlines to protect their existing slots

Hackney/Chelsea Line Proposed tube link between Hackney and Chelsea

Hatfield rail crash Rail crash outside Hatfield in which four passengers were killed and thirty-five injured when a GNER train travelling from London to Leeds derailed on 17 October 2000

HC emissions Hydrocarbon emissions

Heathrow Link Joint rail-link venture between BAA plc and British Railways Board

Highways Agency Executive Agency of the Department of Transport

Hindhead Bypass A3 bypass through area of outstanding natural beauty

Honda Manufacturers of cars, motorcycles and power equipment

IATA International Air Transport Association

Infraco An example of an infraco is a bidding company prepared to take on the responsibility for providing the track and signals and infrastructure of the tube

International Civil Aviation Organisation International air transport association to increase safety and security of international civil aviation

King, John First Chairman of British Airways

Kyoto Protocol Proposed international agreement to cut CO_2 emissions

Ladbroke Grove rail crash Occurred when a Great Western Inter-City Express went through a red signal killing 31 passengers, 5 October 1999

Liverpool and Manchester Railway (1829) First inter-city railway line

Lloyd's Bonds (1860) Bonds issued by Lloyd's of London in 1860

London and North Western (1846) Railway formed after the merger of London and Birmingham, Grand Junction and Manchester and Birmingham Railways

LUL London Underground Limited

M25 Arterial motorway around London

Maglev Technology Magnetic levitation transport

Manchester Ship Canal Canal opened in 1894 to provide access for shipping from the Mersey to Greater Manchester

Marshall, Colin Chairman of Government Task Force on the industrial use of energy

Mayor Ken Livingstone, first elected Mayor of London, elected 4 May 2000

Mayor's transport strategy The Mayor's strategy plan to ease congestion in London over the next ten years

Mercury The first company to be allowed to challenge the BT telephone monopoly in the UK

Midland Railway (1844) Railway merger of York and Midland, Midland Counties, North Midland Rail and the Birmingham and Derby Railways

Modern Ports: UK Policy, November 2000 White paper on future of British Ports

Morton, Sir Alastair First Chairman of the Strategic Rail Authority

National Freight Corporation Privatised freight company, wholly owned by its employees

NATS National Air Traffic Services

NCP National Car Parks

NEB National Enterprise Board

Network Rail Company limited by guarantee by the Secretary of State for Transport to run UK railways within a privatised format whilst embracing some elements of a nationalised industry

NHS National Health Service established in 1948

NOx emissions Nitric oxide and nitrogen oxide combined

Potters Bar rail crash Seven passengers were killed and seventy injured when a WAGN train travelling from King's Cross crashed at Potter's Bar Station on 10 May 2002

Pound Lock A common type of canal lock in the form of a chamber with gates on either side

PPP Public private partnerships

Private Finance Initiative Finance provided from the private sector to fund large capital projects

Rail Executive Committee (1912-1921) Committee convened between 1912-1921 to run the railways under emergency powers

Rail Passengers' Committee, South of England Committee to air the views of rail passengers in the south of England under the guidance of the Railways Act of 1993

Railtrack Company that owned most of the nation's railway infrastructure

Railway Rates Tribunal Established in 1921 to supervise charging of railways

Railways Act (1921) Streamlined railways to four lines and established the Railways Rates Tribunal.

Railways Act (1993) Paved the way for privatisation of the railways

Rainhill Trials Competition held in 1828 to find the best locomotive for the new Liverpool to Manchester Railway

Regulation of the Forces Act (1871) Act passed to transfer control of the armed forces and railways to services of the Crown

Road humps Traffic calming measure

Sangatte Terminal French rail freight terminal close to the Red Cross refugee centre in Northern France

Selsden Park Conference Location of conference chaired by Edward Heath as leader of the Conservative party which welcomed more free enterprise policies

Siemens, Thyssen Krupp and Adtranz Collectively known as

Transrapid, responsible for the building of the high-speed rail link between Beijing and Shanghai

Smith, Andrew Chief Secretary to the Treasury from 11 May 1999 to May 2002

South Sea Bubble A time of massive rises in share prices in the Stock Exchange of early nineteenth century England, when a number of worthless companies saw their prices rise spectacularly, only to crash later

Sputnik Russian space programme, Sputnik 1, first artificial satellite put into orbit in 1957

SRA Strategic Rail Authority

Strowger Automated telephone switching system patented by Alman B. Strowger in 1891

Ten-year plan Department of Environment, Transport and the Regions plan, 'Transport 2010'

TfL Transport for London

Thames Conservancy Body established in 1857 to control the River Thames below Staines

Thames Gateway project Large regeneration project encompassing parts of East London, North Kent and the North Thames Corridor

Thameslink 2000 Project due to be completed in 2006 to upgrade the principal feeder routes into London

Third Way Term attributed to Giddens, Anthony, -'The Renewal of Social Democracy', Polity Press (London) 1991

Thomas Cook Travel company established 1841

Traffic cushion Traffic calming measure

Transport 2010 Otherwise known as the 'Ten-year plan'

Transport Act (1947) Established a British Transport Commission to oversee the regulation of licences

Transport Department Officially known as The Department for Planning and Infrastructure, responsible for the activities of the Department of Transport

Transport Road Research Laboratory Centre for UK transport research

TXE4 Electronic telephone exchange with solid-state processors

Wayleaves Easement or right of way granted by a land or property owner for development

Bibliography

RAILWAYS

CMS Cameron McKenna	Bundle of Documents relating to a Petition for a Railway Administration Order	7.10.01	London
Rail Passengers Ctte for S England	Annual Report 2000-2001	Jan 2002	London
Strategic Rail Authority	The Strategic Plan: summary	Jan 2002	London
Strategic Rail Authority	The Strategic Plan	Jan 2002	London
Rail Passengers Council	Funding the Railways	May 2002	London
Strategic Rail Authority	Towards a Safer, Better, Bigger Railway Annual Report 2000-2001	5.7.01	London
Railtrack	1999 Network Management Statement for Great Britain		London
Modern Railways (James Abbott)	Japan: the home of reliable railways	April 2001	UK
Tanemura Naoki	Trains - The Best Way to Travel		Japan
Nishio Gentarrow	Japan's Railways - Yesterday, today and Tomorrow		Japan
Railways Abroad	Japan - The Realm of the Railways		
Railway Technology.com	Eurostar Italia -High Speed Network Italy	13.12.01	Internet
Tobias Benjamin Kohler	InterCityExpress (ICE) Intercity-NeiTech	2001	Internet www.mercurio.iet.unipi.it (Italy)
Anders Elkberg	Some Facts on the Swedish High Speed Train X2000	12.8.98	Internet www.charmec.chalmers.se (Sweden)
Scientific American (Jean-Claude Raoul)	How Hig-Speed Trains Make Tracks	1997	Internet www.sciam.com

ROADS & CARS

PG Boulter, AJ Hickman, S Latham (TRL Ltd) P Davison, P Whiteham (AEA Technology plc)	The Impacts of traffic Calming Measures on Vehicle Exhaust Emissions	2001	TLR Crowthorne, Berks
DETR	Environmental Impacts of Road Vehicles in Use	July 99	UK
DETR	A New Deal for Trunk Roads in England	July 98	London
DETR	A New Deal for Trunk Roads in England: Guidance on the New Approach to Appraisal	July 98	London
Highways Agency	Annual Report & Accounts	31.01.02	London
DTLR	Traffic Commissioners' Annual Report 2000-2001	Sept 01	London
Highways Agency	Business Plan 2001/02	Feb 01	London
DETR	What Role for Trunk Roads in England? Volume 1	1997	London
DTLR	Powering Future Vehicles Draft Government Strategy	Dec 2001	London
BRF in assoc with Ford Motor Co Ltd	Basic Road Statistics 1999		London
Energy Saving Trust	Pathways to Future Vehicles	April 2002	London

AIR TRANSPORT

DotEcon Ltd	Auctioning Airport Slots	January 2001	London
DETR	The Future of Aviation	Dec 2000	London

WATER TRANSPORT

DTLR	Transport Statistics Report Maritime Statistics 2000	Dec 2001	London
DTLR	Transport Statistics Bulletin Waterborne Freight in the United Kingdom: 2000	Jan 2002	London
British Waterways	Annual Report & Accounts 2000-01	2001	Watford

UNDERGROUND

HoC Transport, Local Government & the Regions Committee	London Underground 2nd Report of Session 2001-02	30.1.02	London
Transport for London	Transport Statistics for London 2001	2002	London
Transport for London	The Case Against PPP	2002	London
Greater London Authority	The Mayor's Transport Strategy	July 01	London
Ernst & Young	London Underground PPPs Value for Money Review	5 Feb 02	London
Transport for London	London Underground Public Private Partnership Executive Summary	21.3.02	London
Mayor of London	Planning for London's Growth	March 02	London
Greater London Authority	The Mayor's Transport Strategy Highlights	July 01	London
London Transport	Annual Report 2000/01	July 2001	London

GENERAL

DETR	Annual Report 2001	March 01	London
National Statistics	Public Expenditure	April 01	London
DETR	Transport 2010 Meeting the Local Transport Challenge	March 01	London
National Statistics	Transport Statistics Bulletin: A Bulletin of Public Transport Statistics: Great Britain 2001 edition	Nov 01	London
DTLR	Transport Statistics Great Britain 2001 Edition	October 01	London
National Statistics	Transport Trends	March 01	London
DETR	Transport 2010 The 10 Year Plan	July 2000	London
National Statistics	Traffic in Great Britain: Q4 2001 Data	Feb 02	London

National Statistics	Transport Statistics Bulletin Transport of Goods by Road in Great Britain: 2000 data	May 2001	London
	Transport Statistics Bulletin: National Travel Survey 1998/2000 update	July 2001	London
Dept of Environment, Dept of Transport	PPG13 A Guide to Better Practice	1999	London
DETR	Transport 2010 The Background Analysis	July 2000	London
Institute of Directors	Transport & Business: the Government's Route	Nov98	London

PRIVATE SECTOR

LPG Autocentres	Driving into the Future	2000	Poole, Dorset
Dart Group plc	Interim Report 2001	15.11.01	Christchurch Dorset
Dart Group plc	Report & Accounts 2001	21.6.01	Christchurch, Dorset
Associated British Port Holdings	Interim Results 2001	4.9.01	London
Stagecoach Holdings plc	Summary Annual Report 2001	2001	Perth
Stagecoach Group	Interim Report 2001	6.12.01	Perth
Sea Containers Ltd	Annual Report 2000	2000	Hamilton, Bermuda
Vehicle Inspectorate	Business Plan 2001/02	London	
NFC	Annual Report & Accounts 1998	London	
Clydeport	Annual Report & Accounts 2001	March 02	Glasgow
Strategic Rail Authority	Freight Quarterly	Spring 2002	London
DTLR	Major Infrastructure projects: delivering a fundamental change	2001	London

Index